INDIAN CULTURE
AND
EUROPEAN
TRADE GOODS

GEORGE IRVING QUIMBY

Madison • Milwaukee • London • 1966

THE UNIVERSITY OF WISCONSIN PRESS

Published by
The University of Wisconsin Press
Madison, Milwaukee, and London
U.S.A.: Box 1379, Madison, Wisconsin 53701
U.K.: 26–28 Hallam Street, London, W. 1
Copyright © 1966
by the Regents of the University of Wisconsin
Printed in the United States of America
by North Central Publishing Co., St. Paul, Minnesota
Library of Congress Catalog Card Number 66-13805

For HELEN
EDWARD
JOHN
ROBERT
SEDNA
HARRY
and CHARLES

PREFACE

This book is a collection of essays which were written separately, over a period of six years or more, but which in combination here make up an anthropologically oriented history of Indian culture from the beginning of the seventeenth century through the first quarter of the nineteenth. These chapters provide a sequel to an earlier book written by me, entitled *Indian Life in the Upper Great Lakes: 11,000 B.C. to A.D. 1800* (University of Chicago Press, 1960). In that book I was most concerned with details of the oldest cultures of the region, and although I summarized the tribal cultures of historic times, I was not then able to provide the kind of information and interpretation of the historic period that is contained in the new book. In fact my realization of what I did not know about the archaeology of the historic period in the upper or western Great Lakes region was the stimulus that led to the writing of the present book. And this book does for the archaeology of the historic period what my previous book did for the prehistoric archaeology of the region. Thus the two books complement each other; the first emphasizes prehistoric cultures, the second emphasizes the historic cultures.

The word *culture* is used here in its specialized sense, as comprehending material objects like tools, weapons, utensils, ornaments, etc., as well as acts, beliefs, attitudes, ideas, customs, and anything else that is dependent upon language, which is a man-made system of communication by symbols. Culture is transmitted from one person to another and from one generation to another. It is the means by which man obtains his food, shelter from the elements, defense against his enemies, and reproduction of his kind. In the period encompassed by this book the Indians of the western Great Lakes changed from a Stone Age type of culture to what was essentially an Iron Age type, most of which was introduced from Europe.

The culture history presented in this book is the product of archaeological research supplemented when possible by eyewitness accounts of European missionaries and traders. Since the Indians themselves left no written record, most of the information about their cultures has been excavated from beneath the earth by trowel or abstracted from the documents of ethnohistory. But no matter where these data came from, they have in common the fact that they are part of an unintentional record of peoples and cultures now extinct, and they are the primary sources of information for the reconstruction of culture history presented in this book.

Compared to what I had hoped to accomplish, this book is little more than a beginning. It does synthesize the existing information, present new data, and provide some new interpretations. More importantly, it may direct other students of the subject into more fruitful avenues of inquiry; or when new data and approaches become available this book can indicate what was known up to 1965, thereby saving considerable time and effort for future investigators.

I am grateful to the Chicago Natural History Museum (formerly Field Museum of Natural History) for providing me with funds for field work and travel, time to write, and necessary facilities. I am also grateful to the American Council of Learned Societies for a grant-in-aid awarded me in 1961–62. Among the archaeologists who kindly allowed me access to their data and ideas were David A. Baerreis, Lewis R. Binford, Leland R. Cooper, Helen Devereux, J. Norman Emerson, Robert L. Hall, Elaine Bluhm Herold, Robert Hruska, Ronald J. Mason, Moreau Maxwell, Alan L. McPherron, Warren L. Wittry, and James V. Wright. Among the institutions which graciously permitted me to study their collections were the Delta County Historical Society Museum, Escanaba, Michigan; the Grand Rapids Public Museum; the Illinois State Museum; the Madeline Island Historical Museum, La Pointe, Wisconsin; the Museum of Anthropology of the University of Michigan; the Michigan State University Museum; the Milwaukee Public Museum; the National Museum of Canada; the Neville Museum, Green Bay, Wisconsin; the Oshkosh (Wisconsin) Public Museum; the Royal Ontario Museum; the St. Joseph Historical Museum, Niles, Michigan; the University of Illinois; and the University of Toronto.

Parts of four chapters of this book have appeared previously, in the *Chicago Natural History Museum Bulletin*, the *Michigan Archaeologist, Michigan History, Ethnohistory*, and *Miscellanea Paul Rivet, Octogenario Dicata* (XXXI Congreso Internacional de Americanistas). The drawings used in this book were made under my supervision and are the very able work of Gustaf Dalstrom, artist in the Department of Anthropology, Chicago Natural History Museum. The best of the photographs were made by John Bayalis and Homer V. Holdren. The remainder were supplied by me or are from old files in the Museum.

Lastly, I should like to acknowledge my debt to James R. Getz, Field Associate in Anthropology at the Chicago Natural History Museum, a tireless walker, with whom I have explored considerable portions of western Great Lakes shore lines during the past seven years.

G. I. Q.

Chicago Natural History Museum
Chicago, Illinois
January, 1965

CONTENTS

ILLUSTRATIONS

INDIAN CULTURE AND
EUROPEAN TRADE GOODS

CHAPTER 1

INTRODUCTION

In the early part of the seventeenth century French explorers and fur traders arrived in the western Great Lakes region bringing with them a European culture. This culture was obviously superior to the Stone Age culture of the Indians, particularly in the broad field of mechanics; but in concepts of wisdom, virtue, ethics, and justice the aboriginal culture was essentially equal to that of the invaders (see Josephy *et al.*, 1961, p. 244). By and large the meeting of French and Indian was a confrontation of Stone Age culture by Iron Age culture. And ultimately the culture contact engendered by the fur trade destroyed the aboriginal culture, so that by the twentieth century there remained only an empty shell of what had existed at the time of discovery.

Samuel de Champlain, the founder of Quebec, reached the eastern shore of Lake Huron in 1615, and it is likely that Etienne Brulé had seen Lake Michigan and Lake Superior by 1622. In 1634, Jean Nicolet journeyed westward along the north shore of Lake Huron, through the Straits of Mackinac, and along the north shore of Lake Michigan to a place along the shores of Green Bay. There he astonished the Indian residents by appearing in a robe of China damask profusely decorated with flowers and birds of various colors and carrying two pistols. These he fired into the air, causing the Indians to believe that he carried thunder in his hands. The terror-stricken women and children fled the scene, but returned in time to attend a feast in honor of Nicolet, at which 120 beavers were eaten.

Medard Chouart des Groseilliers made an important journey into the region in the years between 1654 and 1656, during which he explored and traded in the northern Lake Michigan area. On that particular trek Des Groseilliers did not reach Lake Superior, although later, in 1658–59, accompanied by Pierre Esprit Radisson, he did include the Lake Superior area in his trading activities and explorations. Many French traders, explorers, and missionaries followed Des Groseilliers and Radisson, among them Marquette and Joliet, La Salle and his associates, Du Lhut, and Nicolas Perrot, Allouez, Dreuillettes, and Dablon. By 1680 the French seem to have been well established throughout the western Great Lakes region. Even before this date the region was permeated with *coureurs de bois*, or unlicensed traders; *hivernants*, those remaining in the interior but in the employ of traders; and *voyageurs*, the *engagés* of the licensed traders. In 1680 there were already forty-five Frenchmen settled at Michilimackinac (Fig. 1).

Fig. 1. — Drawing reconstructing Michilimackinac (St. Ignace) as it was in the days of Father Hennepin. Courtesy of Chicago Natural History Museum.

How did the Indians regard these foreign intruders? At first they felt astonishment and awe. Certainly, too, they had a high regard for the superior tools, utensils, and weapons of the white men. Also there were the stories brought back by Indians who had been sent to France as hostages or curiosities and then returned to the western Great Lakes region. One such Indian, a Huron, reported to his friends and relatives that he had seen the golden cabin of the French king rolling along the ground, pulled by eight moose without horns, and that he also had seen a wonderful machine which spoke and told the time of day. The Indians did not consider the French to be handsome. They disliked the white skins and curly hair and thought beards were loathsome. Their own skins, well oiled and relatively hairless, were more soft and delicate than those of the white men. By comparison with himself the Indian usually considered the Frenchmen ugly and rude.

How did the Frenchmen regard the Indians? There probably were great differences of attitude. For instance, the unlettered peasants who became the *coureurs de bois* had a great deal in common with the Indians. At the other extreme was the educated urban Frenchman who kept a diary or journal. To represent this point of view I have chosen to quote from the works of Father Louis Hennepin, a Recollect missionary who was one of La Salle's associates. Father Hennepin (1698, Part 2, pp. 119–21) wrote:

The savages have very little regard to the rules of civility, in use among the Europeans; nay, they even fall a laughing, when they see our People employed in paying mutual respects one to another. Upon their arrival at a place, they scarce even trouble themselves with saluting the company there present, but sit squat on the tail, without giving any manner of salutation, or so much as looking upon anyone, although a visit were made to them. They sometimes run into the first hut that lies in their way, without speaking one word; take place where they can; and afterward light their pipe or reed: Thus they smoke in profound silence, and then depart after the same manner. When they enter our houses, built and furnished after the European fashion, they get possession of the principal post, but if a chair be set on the middle of the hearth, they immediately seize upon it, and never rise up, to give place to any man whatsoever, although he were even a prince or king; For they take as much state upon themselves as can be done by persons of the highest rank and quality.

In the northern countries, the *savage* men and women take care to cover their privy parts, all the rest of their body being destitute of cloaths. The southern savages go stark naked, without any sense of shame; nay, they make no scruple to break wind publickly, having no regard to the presence of any person whatever. They treat their elders very rudely, when they do not sit in council, and the common discourse both of the men and women is incessantly full of ribaldry and obscene expressions. As for the kindly correspondence between them, they generally endeavour to conceal it; nevertheless, they sometimes take so little precaution in that affair, that they are often surprized: Besides, the *savages* observe none of the rules of that natural modesty and civil deportment which are in use among us, between persons of both sexes; neither are they accustomed to any of the caresses or regular methods of courtship, which are usually performed by the civilized people of *Europe*; but every thing is there transacted in a gross manner, and with a great deal of brutishness. They never wash their wooden or bark dishes, nor their porrengers and spoons; nay, the *savage* women after having turned their young children dry with their fingers, wipe them very lightly with a piece of rind [birch bark], and then immediately fall about handling their victuals. Indeed, this nastiness was often very offensive to me, and even hindered me from eating with those people in the hut, where they had made me an invitation; neither do they scarce at any time wash their hands or face.

The children shew very little respect to their parents, nay, they often are so audacious as to beat them, without receiving due correction for such misdemeanours; by reason that (according to their maxim) blows would serve only to balk their courage, and to render them uncapable of being good soldiers. They sometimes eat snorting and blowing like brute beasts, and as soon as the men have entered a hut, they fall to smoking tobacco: If a covered pot happen to lie in their way, they make no scruple to uncover it, to see what may be contained therein: They eat in a dish that the Dogs have licked without washing or scouring it, and when they light on fat meat, they only rub their faces, and haste with their hands to cleanze them, not forbearing to belch incessantly.

Those *savages* who have found means to truck for shirts with the *Europeans* never take care to wash them, but generally let them rot on their backs: They seldom pare their nails, and scarce ever wash their meat before they dress it. Their huts in the north country are for the most part very nasty. I was also much surprised one day to see an old decrepit woman, who was employed in biting a child's hair, and devouring the lice that were in it. The women are not ashamed to make water before any company, yet they chuse to go a mile or two into the woods to ease their bodies, rather than to expose themselves to the publick view; when the children have fouled their cloaths, they usually throw off the urine with their hands. These people are also often seen eating as their lie upon the ground like dogs. In a word, these people are unwilling to put themselves to the least trouble upon any account whatever, and act on all occasions after a very brutish manner.

However, notwithstanding all this strange barbarousness, many things are transacted by them with a great deal of discretion and agreeableness.

When any one happens to come into their huts, whilst they are eating, they usually set before him their dishes full of meat, and they take it as a very great favour, when every thing is eaten up, that was presented, nay, they would chuse rather to be destitute of Provisions two days, than to let you depart, without offering to you every thing they have, with much sincerity; so that if the messes [units of food] happen to be already distributed, upon the arrival of any person, the good woman, whose right it is to make this distribution, finds means to order matters after such a manner, that there may be somewhat to be given to those who come unlooked for. Some of these *savages* presented to us the finest mats, and set us in the best place of the hut, when we came to make them a visit, and those who have often conversed with the *Europeans* are wont to salute us when we meet them. It is also customary among the same people, when they have received a present, to send back part thereof to those who make it.

Although they are accustomed to treat their elders after a rude manner, nevertheless they have a great deal of respect and deference for their counsels, following them exactly and acknowledging that their old men have more experience, and are better versed in the management of affairs than they.

So much for the French view as expressed by Father Hennepin. He personally encountered Indians of a number of different tribes, and his appraisal, even if possibly plagiarized, has the smell of truth to it.

The arrival of the French in the western Great Lakes region in the seventeenth century not only marked the end of the long prehistoric period but also the beginning of the relatively brief historic period. For purposes of convenience in the manipulation of the available information I have divided the historic period into three temporal segments: (1) the Early Historic period, from about A.D. 1610 to 1670, (2) the Middle Historic period, from 1670 to 1760, and (3) the Late Historic period, from 1760 to 1820 or slightly later. This division seems to work well in the western Great Lakes region and probably is applicable to much of the Mississippi Valley. It would not necessarily be applicable to other regions.

In 1935, while still a student at the University of Michigan, I began a study of Late Historic period archaeological sites in the western Great Lakes region with the assumption that such a study would bridge the gaps between knowledge of tribal cultures obtained ethnologically and knowledge of prehistoric cultures that had been gained through the efforts of archaeologists. I had hoped that I could use the direct historical method of starting with known

tribal groups and could work back from the known into the unknown realms of prehistory by means of either stratigraphy or
typology of traits of material culture, or both. I had read enough
ethnology to realize that I could not achieve my aims by starting
with the period covered by existing ethnological monographs or
museum collections dating after 1850. Therefore, I would have to
concentrate first on archaeological collections representative of Indians who lived in the region around A.D. 1800.

As reported in a subsequent chapter, the association of trade
silver ornaments with Indian cultural remains from archaeological
excavations proved to be the best single criterion for dating sites
of the Late Historic period. Accordingly, cultural materials from a
number of such sites were studied and analyzed, but unfortunately
the results desired were not obtained. I discovered that by 1760
the Indians of the western Great Lakes region had become so
changed by employment in the fur trade and contact with the culture of white men that the significant typological continuities in
material culture had been destroyed. For instance, where I had expected to find pottery and arrowheads in a dated Ottawa village site
there were brass kettles instead of pottery and lead balls for flintlock guns instead of flint arrowheads. There were iron axes instead
of stone celts, and white kaolin pipes instead of stone or clay pipes
of native manufacture. In short, the kinds of aboriginal cultural
materials that I wished to use for identification and comparison
were no longer being made after 1760; thus it was impossible to
employ the direct historical method using Late Historic period
archaeological assemblages as a starting point. If the gaps between
history and prehistory in the western Great Lakes region were to
be closed it would have to be undertaken with identifiable tribal
cultures of the Middle or Early Historic periods (prior to 1760)
as a starting point.

Despite the fact that the Late Historic period, 1760–1820, did
not turn out to be useful in the way I had hoped, it was nonetheless
interesting and fruitful in its own right. The study of the remains
of tribal culture of the period suggested that the fur trade and contact with white men had produced a cultural uniformity in the material culture of various tribal groups — a kind of Pan-Indian
culture throughout the western Great Lakes region. Moreover, the
material culture of this period is in itself a record of cultural

change, manifestations of processes of acculturation that had been in operation for more than a hundred years. The groups of Indians whose culture was changing because of contact with Western civilization made and/or used certain artifacts that reflected processes of cultural change and translated it into practically imperishable form. The categories of change reflected in these artifacts are as follows:

New types of artifacts received through trade or other contact channels. — In this category are such things as flintlock guns, gunflints, gun worms, bullets and shot, bullet molds, iron knives of various kinds, steel traps, iron hoes, iron axes, woolen blankets, cloth of various kinds, articles of clothing, awls and needles of steel, scissors, brass thimbles, various kinds and sizes of kettles made of brass or tin, European and oriental chinawares, glass bottles, European patent medicines such as Essence of Peppermint and Turlington's "Balsom of Life," burning glasses and steel strike-a-lights, tobacco pipes of kaolin, iron fishhooks and spear points, jew's-harps, vermilion face and body paint, glass beads, various kinds of silver ornaments, and a host of tools, weapons, utensils, clothing, and ornaments, many of which would have been in use among some or all groups of contemporary white people. However, some of these new types of artifacts were made specifically for trade with Indians and were not used by white men. For example, the crescent-shaped gorget of silver with totemic designs engraved upon it was worn only by Indians, although a similar gorget differently engraved was worn by military men. The circular gorget with engraved designs was copied from the native form in shell and was produced by white silversmiths solely for use by Indians. A similar example is the wampum that consisted of small tubular beads of glass or shell manufactured by white men only for use in the fur trade. To a somewhat lesser degree, even the flintlock guns with the serpent-shaped sideplates of brass and the enlarged trigger guards were made specifically for use by Indians. Hair-pullers made of brass springs, tomahawk pipes, and shell runtees are also examples of new types of artifacts made by white men especially for use by Indians. Artifacts in this subcategory were uniquely a part of Indian culture despite the fact that they were originated by white men, and in this respect they were different from those new types of artifacts accepted by Indians but also in use among white people.

New types of artifacts of forms copied from introduced models, but reproduced locally of native materials by native manufacture. — In this category are various items such as stone pipes made in imitation of the kaolin trade pipes, some bone combs copied from imported bone combs, wooden yokes for carrying burdens made in imitation of European shoulder yokes, molds made of local stone for the casting of lead bullets or lead buttons and ornaments, skin clothing modeled after imported types, and probably maple sugar, the production of which seemingly was based on the use of imported utensils for boiling and a knowledge of the sugar produced from cane syrup.

New types of artifacts of introduced forms, made and/or decorated locally, partly from native materials and partly from imported materials. — This category includes cloth shirts, blankets, or articles of imported clothing that are decorated with beads or dyed porcupine quills or painted designs; skin clothing patterned after European styles but ornamented with painted, beaded, or quill-work designs; hand mirrors with locally made frames and handles; iron awls with native handles of wood or bone; leather bullet pouches decorated with glass beads or dyed quill-work; and trunks made of rawhide.

New types of artifacts of introduced forms, manufactured locally from imported materials through the use of an introduced technique or a native technique similar to the introduced one. — In this category are items such as sashes and garters woven of imported yarns, clothing of European style made of imported cloth, and some silver ornaments made from silver cut from imported ornaments.

Old types of artifacts modified by the substitution of an imported material for a local material that was inferior in physical properties, lacking in prestige, or harder to obtain. — This category contains such things as certain kinds of woven bags made of imported wool yarns instead of spun bast fiber or buffalo hair; tinkling cones, tubular beads, and hair pipes made of brass kettle fragments instead of native copper; clothing of native style made of imported cloth; courting flutes made of worn-out gun barrels; triangular arrowheads and end-scrapers chipped of bottle glass instead of flint; triangular arrowheads made locally of sheet brass or iron; gaming counters made of broken chinaware; and headdresses and ornaments made with imported feathers of tropical birds and dyed horsehair. The forms have not changed, but the material of manufacture is new.

Old types of artifacts modified by the substitution of either imported material or heretofore unused local material, the use of which involves a different technological principle to achieve a similar end product. — This category includes items such as elbow pipes of catlinite ornamented with designs inlaid in molten lead and scrapers made of sheet brass from kettles but curved to add the necessary strength to the metal.

Old types of artifacts modified by the introduction of a new element of subject matter. — In this category of cultural change there are such things as birchbark scrolls with representations of European objects or symbols engraved upon them, rock paintings in which the pictographs depict European objects or symbols, and any other items in which the method of manufacture and style remain unchanged although the subject matter represents a new element.

Most examples of cultural change by means of acculturation fall into the first category, which was new types of artifacts received through trade or other contact channels. There were, however, many examples of cultural change belonging to the fifth category, which was old types of artifacts modified by the substitution of an imported material. This category of change as manifested in the Late Historic period, 1760–1820, seems to be a reflection of cultural conservatism, whereas in the Early Historic period, 1610–1760, it is primarily a manifestation of innovation. At some future time when more data are available, it should be possible to analyze each culture and period in terms of category and quantity of culture change as well as the rate of change. Such analysis might provide characterizations of culture pattern and process which are not apparent at the present time. What we really need now are more sites of the Early and Middle Historic periods, and careful archaeological exploration of such sites.

Within the last twenty-five years, and particularly the last ten years, an increase in interest in historic period archaeology plus availability of new data obtained through excavation has made possible a beginning, at least, in the interpretation of the archaeology of the historic period. The new data particularly concern the critical periods of time prior to 1760 when enough of the aboriginal culture remained to provide information that archaeologists could use to connect the historic cultural entities to the long continuum of prehistoric cultures in the western Great Lakes region.

REFERENCES

Josephy *et al.*, 1961; Hennepin, 1698.

CHAPTER 2

___

THE FIRST TWELVE THOUSAND YEARS

The upper or western Great Lakes region consists of Lake Michigan, Lake Huron, Lake Superior, and all the lands surrounding them and draining into them through rivers, streams, and creeks. It is a vast region, encompassing more than 200,000 square miles of land and water, most of which lie in Ontario, Michigan, and Wisconsin (Fig. 2). Elsewhere (Quimby, 1960) I have described the succession of glacial advances and retreats and the multitude of glacial and postglacial lake stages and changing environments that took place between the end of the Pleistocene epoch and the beginning of the Christian Era. Only in the last part of its long geologic history did the western Great Lakes become the kind of region it was at the time of the arrival of French explorers and missionaries.

In the northern part there were the undulating rock surfaces of the Canadian Shield, old mountains ground smooth by the action of glaciers on a continental scale. In the southern part of the region there were the soils composed of sands, clays, and gravels deposited by the glaciers or the waters flowing from them. In the northern part of the region coniferous trees dominated the landscape in most places, and in the southern portions the deciduous hardwoods domi-

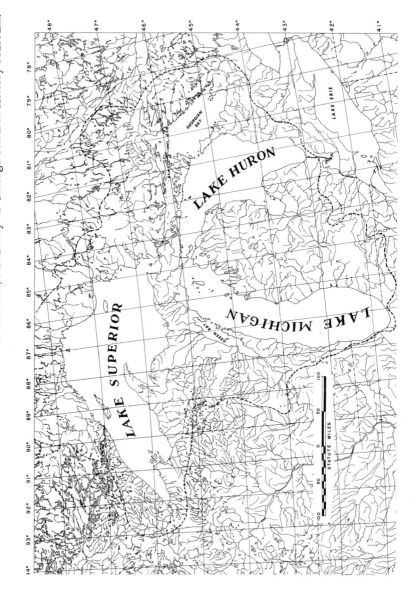

Fig. 2. — Map of the western or upper Great Lakes region (area enclosed by dotted line). Courtesy of Chicago Natural History Museum.

nated the scene. In the middle areas there were varying admixtures of hardwoods and conifers.

Water, especially in the northern half of the region, was the most important single factor of the geography. The lakes and rivers were the main highways that were used in spring, summer, and autumn for travel by canoe. The giant sweep of the shore lines of the western Great Lakes constituted an almost endless river, the main trunk line of voyaging for birchbark canoes. The smaller lakes and rivers were the feeder roads and connecting highways. From the waters of the Great Lakes came the several species of large fish, the only animal food present in an abundance sufficient to nourish the summer villages of the non-farming bands of Indians. Probably the sturgeon alone was so plentiful at many places that Indian families returning from the isolation of the winter hunting grounds could unite in large numbers to form a summer village at a sturgeon fishery.

American Indians had lived in the western Great Lakes region for thousands of years before the arrival of French explorers, traders, and missionaries in the seventeenth century, at the beginning of the Early Historic period. In fact the first humans known to have settled in the region were the Paleo-Indian hunters of large game animals who arrived there in late glacial times between 11,000 and 9,000 B.C. They used spears tipped with specialized forms of large fluted points made of chipped flint and chalcedony (Fig. 3). Points such as these have been found only south of the line marking the maximum advance of the Valders glacier, and on the landward side of the former beach of glacial Lake Algonquin. This distribution of fluted points is essentially the same as that of the remains of mastodons, some of which have been dated by means of the radiocarbon method at approximately 11,000 to 7,500 B.C. It looks as if the Paleo-Indians of the western Great Lakes region hunted these elephants just as similar Paleo-Indians did in western North America during the same period. In any case, the Paleo-Indians of the western Great Lakes and the mastodons lived in the region at the same time.

When these first Indian settlers lived in the western Great Lakes the climate was cooler than now. Spruce forests were common, but there were also stands of hardwoods and pines in favorable locations. Besides the mastodons there were other large animals now extinct, such as the giant beaver and a large deer. Barren-ground caribou and elk were also present and probably a number of other animals, many of which still live in parts of the region.

By about 8,000 B.C. the region was occupied by various groups of Indians representative of the Aqua-Plano cultural stage. They too were hunters, and used large lanceolate spear points of chipped flint and other kinds of stone. There were a number of different styles of spear points, most of which had parallel sides and pronounced parallel flaking (Fig. 3). These Indian hunters mostly lived north of the line marking the maximum advance of the Valders glacier; thus it looks as if they had moved northward in the region as the Valders ice retreated. Their best-known sites lie on or in the fossil beaches of the postglacial lake stages following glacial Lake Algonquin. This was a period of falling water levels the like of which has not been seen in the region since then. In the Lake Michigan basin the total drop in water level was about 375 feet; in the Lake Huron basin, 425 feet; and in the Lake Superior basin, more than 250 feet.

Coexisting with the Aqua-Plano Indians, but living generally south of the line marking the maximum advance of the Valders glacier, were other groups of Indians who used chipped flint spear points somewhat like those of the Paleo-Indians who preceded them in this area. The spear points in question were relatively short and broad leaf-shaped forms with incurved bases that had been thinned by chipping so that they superficially appeared to be fluted (Fig. 3). The Indian hunters who used these spear points may well have been descendants of the earlier Paleo-Indians who used fluted points and had lived formerly in the same area.

By about 4,000 B.C. the culture of the Aqua-Plano Indians and their contemporaries had changed to or had been superseded by Early Archaic culture. The groups of Indians inhabiting the region were still hunters and they still used lanceolate spear points of chipped flint, although without parallel flaking; but they also used side-notched spear points (Fig. 3). At this time the water levels of the upper Great Lakes were rising, but still destined to go higher, and the climate had become warm. In fact from sometime shortly before 4,000 B.C. until 1,000 B.C. the climate of the western Great Lakes was the warmest it has ever been since the Ice Age. In this long hot period the deciduous hardwood forests and grassy prai-

Fig. 3. — Changes in stone weapon points from about 11,000 B.C. to A.D. 1600. The earliest type is the spear point shown at the bottom. The latest types are the arrowheads in the top row. Courtesy of Chicago Natural History Museum.

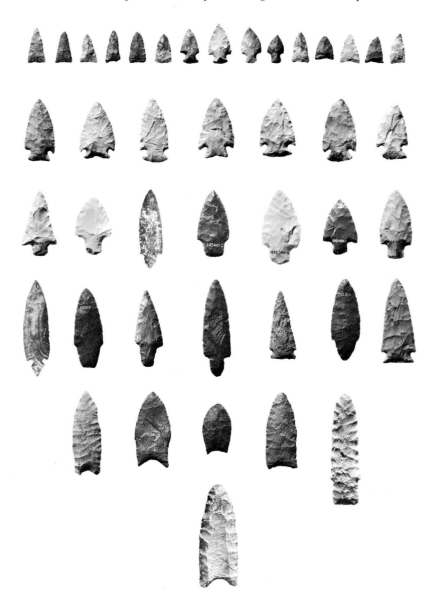

ries achieved their greatest expansion. And in this period there came about the flowering of the forest-oriented Archaic culture.

By about 3,000 B.C. the region was inhabited only by Indians who represented various divisions of the Boreal Archaic group of cultures. An outstanding innovation of Boreal Archaic was the appearance of wood-working tools such as the adze, the gouge, and the grooved axe. These tools were made of hard, non-glassy rock, such as granite, gabbro, and diabase, by means of pecking and grinding with hammerstones and rocks of similar hardness. The pecking and grinding process itself was an innovation, because heretofore stone tools and weapons had been made by flaking and chipping techniques applied to lithic materials of glassy composition.

These Indians used spear-throwers equipped with polished stone weights called banner stones. Their darts and spears were tipped with stemmed, notched, and lanceolate points of chipped flint. They also had scraping tools, knives, and drills of chipped flint. Like all other Archaic Indians they lived by hunting, fishing, and food collecting. Nothing yet is known about their dwellings, but they probably lived in wigwams consisting of a framework of saplings covered by skins or bark.

A unique division of Boreal Archaic was the Old Copper culture, so named because its Indian carriers used raw copper for the manufacture of specific kinds of knives, spear points, socketed axes, gouges, pikes, and awls. The raw copper was picked up in detached chunks that occurred sporadically throughout the region or was mined in the Lake Superior district, particularly on Isle Royale and Keweenaw Peninsula. The copper was not melted and cast in molds, but instead was worked — cold-hammered into the desired shape and heated from time to time in order to keep it from becoming too brittle. The Old Copper Indians were the first in the New World to make objects of metal. Long before the Indians of Peru and Mexico, or for that matter the peoples of England and France, knew the use of metal, the Old Copper Indians were fabricating tools and weapons of copper. They also made grooved and fluted axes of ground and polished stone, and knives, spear points, and scrapers of chipped stone.

The Old Copper Indians were also the first people known to have had dogs in the region. Their dogs were of two kinds, a small one about the size of a coyote and a large one similar in size to the largest Eskimo dogs of modern times.

About 3,000 B.C., or shortly afterward, the waters in the Lake Michigan and Lake Huron basins rose to planes 25 feet above their modern levels. Although there must have been considerable difference in environment from area to area, in general the deciduous hardwoods were dominant over most of the region and the climate was much warmer than the present one until about 1,000 B.C. Among the animals hunted by Archaic Indians were barren-ground caribou, elk, lynx, and probably moose and deer.

Beginning about 1,000 B.C., or slightly later, there was a flowering of Late Archaic culture oriented around religious ideas and manifested by elaborate burial practices. The dead were placed in graves often lined with powdered red ocher and were accompanied by tools, weapons, and ornaments. Such graves might'contain large quantities of short leaf-shaped points of chipped flint, delicate "turkey-tail" blades of blue-gray flint (Fig. 3), copper awls, large daggerlike, lanceolate blades of whitish flint, copper celts (ungrooved flat axes), lanceolate and stemmed lanceolate blades of copper, large quantities of beads made of imported ocean shells, birdstones, thick spheroidal beads of rolled copper sheet, and gorgets or chest ornaments of ground and polished stone. Some of the cemeteries of this variant of Late Archaic culture are associated with old beach lines that follow the Algoma Lake stage in the western Great Lakes. Cemeteries representative of another variant of Late Archaic culture were placed generally in gravelly knolls or kames. The burial furniture included ornaments made of imported ocean shell that had been cut and ground into a shape like the sole of a sandal or moccasin. Such burial sites lacked "turkey-tail" blades and the daggerlike lanceolate knives but often included the other Late Archaic traits listed previously.

At about 600 B.C. there was an important change in the Indian cultures of the western Great Lakes region. To a residual group of Late Archaic traits and characteristics there were added new customs and artifacts involving the manufacture and use of pottery and the construction of burial mounds. These new things did not necessarily arrive in the region at the same time, nor are they necessarily found together, but the mere presence of either pottery or a burial mound in conjunction with traits of Late Archaic style is indicative of the beginning of the period of Early Woodland culture in the western Great Lakes region.

The first pottery of the Early Woodland period was unusually thick, made of clay mixed with particles of granitic rock, and covered inside and outside with impressions of fabric or of a cord-wrapped instrument applied while the clay was still plastic. The typical vessel shape was that of an open-mouth jar or pot with nearly straight sides and a somewhat pointed bottom. The first burial mounds were low, dome-shaped piles of earth or sand erected over one or more grave pits. Not much is known about Early Woodland in the western Great Lakes region, but in my opinion the Indians of that period were not as numerous as the Late Archaic Indians had been. Possibly there was considerable overlapping of the two culture types, with Early Woodland Indians constituting an elite minority in the region. But like the Late Archaic Indians the Early Woodland peoples, here at least, also made their living by hunting, fishing, and food collecting.

About 100 B.C., perhaps somewhat earlier, there was a radical shift in the subsistence pattern of the Indians who lived in the southern part of the region. A limited type of corn agriculture had been introduced by northward moving Hopewell Indians who were the culturally dominant people of the Middle Woodland period.

The Hopewell Indians had already established great ceremonial centers in the Ohio, Mississippi, and Illinois river valleys, where there were large populations of these people. The Illinois Valley type of Hopewell culture had been extended into the western Great Lakes region via the Kankakee River Valley. From this extension were derived the three Hopewell divisions of western Michigan. The first and oldest of these three divisions occupied the valley of the St. Joseph River. The next oldest and most spectacular Hopewell assemblage in the western Great Lakes region was located in the lower Grand River Valley, and the last and also somewhat decadent Hopewellian center was in the lower Muskegon River Valley.

The Hopewell Indians raised corn and squash (pumpkins probably) and also hunted and fished. They preferred riverine situations in prairie and hardwood environments. These Indians engaged in widespread trading activities, by means of which they obtained sea shells from the Gulf of Mexico, raw copper and silver from

Lake Superior, chunks of lead and rock crystals from Missouri and Arkansas, sheet mica from the middle Atlantic Coast, and black obsidian from the Rocky Mountains. From these exotic materials they made elaborate tools, weapons, and ornaments, great quantities of which were lavished on the dead.

Large burial mounds of earth were erected over the deceased, who often were placed in tombs beneath the floor level of the mound. The dead Indians were dressed in cloth robes adorned with ornaments of sheet copper and mica and accompanied by well-made stone knives, copper axes or adzes, Panpipes of copper or silver, stone tobacco pipes with bowls carved realistically in the form of animals or humans, excellent pottery, and many other objects. In the Grand River Valley there were between fifty and sixty-five Hopewell burial mounds distributed among three or more different sites.

Hopewell culture manifested the peak of artistic and technological achievement in the western Great Lakes region. Its essential development took place elsewhere, and it is possible that a climatic deterioration was responsible for the decline of western Great Lakes Hopewell culture. In any case the culture of these Hopewell Indians had disappeared by the beginning of the Late Woodland period, *circa* A.D. 800.

The Late Woodland period was a time of cultural diversity at a relatively uniform level. To judge from the number of known sites it was also the period of maximum aboriginal population. Those Indians who lived in the southern half of the region made their living by farming, hunting, and fishing, whereas those Indians dwelling in the north, beyond the limits of corn growth, depended for their livelihood upon hunting, fishing, and collecting wild food plants.

All of the various groups of Indians of the Late Woodland period possessed pottery. Generally this pottery was made of clay mixed with small particles of granitic rock, but a few groups who entered the region at the beginning of this period preferred to mix crushed shell with the clay from which they made their jars and pots. Tobacco pipes were elbow-shaped or trumpet-shaped and made of fired clay, or were vaselike or disklike and made of stone.

Bows and arrows were used for hunting. Arrowheads, usually of triangular form, were made of chipped flint. Various kinds of scrapers, knives, and drills were also made of chipped flint. Some small knives and awls were made of copper. Other awls, needles, and weaving tools were made of bone. The common axe of the period was a small, ungrooved form made of ground stone.

Clothing usually was made of animal skins, and dwellings were various forms of wigwams or houses made of pole frameworks covered with animal skins or bark from trees or tightly woven mats.

Some areal variations of interest in this period include the building of effigy mounds — low mounds in the shape of animal, human, or mythical creatures — in Wisconsin; circular, enclosed embankments of earth in Michigan; and palisaded villages in Ontario.

At the end of the Late Woodland period the French explorers and traders first arrived in the region. And it is the latter part of this period that only lately has begun to be known through archaeological research. In recent years archaeologists have aimed some of their efforts at delineating the specific cultures of later Late Woodland, because it is these late cultures that ultimately can be connected to known tribal groupings of the historic period.

REFERENCE

Quimby, 1960.

CHAPTER 3

INDIAN CULTURE JUST BEFORE THE FRENCH

In the previous chapter I have reviewed briefly some 12,000 years of the prehistory of the western Great Lakes. But what is the archaeological picture of the region a few years before dawn broke on the historic horizon, just before the French explorers and traders entered the area? Archaeologists really know very little about it, but here are some of the things we do know.

In the closing decades of the sixteenth century or the opening years of the seventeenth century there was a large village and adjacent burial ground bordering a small tributary of the Pentwater River in the western part of central Michigan. There, on a sandy plain, surrounded by virgin forest, lived the Indians whose remains and discards constitute the unintentional record from which archaeologists have reconstructed the Dumaw Creek culture. Although this culture is interesting enough in itself, what makes it important here is time.

Like many other cultures in the region, Dumaw Creek is recognizable as Late Woodland on typological grounds alone. But a dating of this culture by means of the radiocarbon method shows that it belongs to the terminal portion of the Late Woodland period. It is therefore, at the present writing, a rare phenomenon, because it is one of the very few cultures that can be proven to have been in existence just before the French arrived in the region. Undoubtedly there were a number of such cultures, but until they have been dated we cannot be certain that they belong to the very latest part of the Woodland period, an interval that is critical for the archaeological and historical problems explored in this book.

The radiocarbon dating of Dumaw Creek materials was undertaken at the University of Michigan through the kindness of their Radiocarbon Laboratory.* This dating was based on measurement of a "witch's brew" of organic remains consisting of human hair, animal fur and hair, and fragments of human and animal tissue found in one of the graves in the burial ground. In the laboratory this material was treated chemically in preparation for the radiocarbon measurement, upon which is based the date of 1680, plus or minus seventy-five years. In other words, the true date should fall somewhere between A.D. 1605 and 1755. The plus side of this radiocarbon date is too young. For one thing, the burial that was dated lay beneath a white pine stump that was 30 inches in diameter. In this particular area a stump of that diameter is considered indicative of a fully mature tree, which in the case of white pine would suggest an age of 250 to 300 years. The trees in this part of Michigan were cut about 1880, and if this particular tree were 275 years old, it would imply that the Indian burial beneath it was in place slightly after 1600. Another reason for believing that the Dumaw Creek culture dates from about 1600 instead of 1680 is the absence of any trade goods or other evidence of contact with

* The radiocarbon method of dating was developed some years ago by Dr. Willard F. Libby, then of the University of Chicago. It determines the approximate age of organic substances by measuring with special apparatus the amount of carbon 14 they contain. Carbon 14 is a radioactive heavy form of carbon, which is created constantly in the earth's upper atmosphere and subsequently becomes part of the lower atmosphere where it enters all living things. All living matter contains a constant proportion of carbon 14; thus at the time of death of a plant or animal the percentage of carbon 14 in its tissues is known; and since carbon 14 then disintegrates at a known rate, the amount of carbon 14 remaining at any given moment is proportional to the time elapsed since death. By the use of proper samples, technique, equipment, and the application of the radiocarbon principle, it is possible to measure the approximate age of organic remains and the things with which they are associated. It was in this manner that the organic materials with a Dumaw Creek burial were dated.

Europeans. Trade goods seem to have been present in the eastern part of the upper Great Lakes region by 1620, and I would expect that a few, at least, would have filtered into western Michigan via channels of aboriginal trade or contact.

The Indians who were the product of Dumaw Creek culture made their living by farming, hunting, and gathering. They raised pumpkins and most probably corn. Animals that they hunted included elk, deer, beaver, raccoon, bear, buffalo, and weasel. They collected wild grapes and probably many other edible plants. Their farming implements, which have not survived them, probably consisted of wooden digging sticks and bone or shell hoes hafted to wooden handles, because such was the case with their contemporaries elsewhere. Their principal hunting weapon was the bow and arrow. Arrows were tipped with thin triangular points of chipped flint and ranged in length from about .5 to 1.5 inches. They probably also used spears tipped with larger flint points, and snares of various kinds.

In making these arrowheads, the first step was to find a suitable pebble or small cobble of flint. This raw flint was placed on an anvil — probably a flat stone in this case — and then struck with a hammerstone. The blow was directed parallel to the vertical axis of the pebble in such a way that as the pebbles shattered from the impact it produced numerous uncontrolled flakes and a distinctive type of bipolar core. Suitable flakes were then selected and chipped into triangular points. In many instances when a part of the flake was the right shape and thickness it was left alone and only chipped where necessary to obtain the proper form and sharpness. Such points (Fig. 4) have been found by the hundreds at the Dumaw Creek site, and it is likely that it took only a few minutes for a skilled flint-knapper to make one of these arrowheads. The arrow shafts were made of wood sanded smooth by grooved sandstone tablets used in pairs. The flint arrowheads were fastened into a slot at the outer end of the shaft and held in place by tight wrappings of sinew. The opposite end of the shaft was notched and feathered. Their bows were made of wood and strung with twisted sinew or leather strings.

Although we have not found the remains of Dumaw Creek houses, the known dwelling types of Late Woodland and historic times are limited in this region to long-houses or several styles of

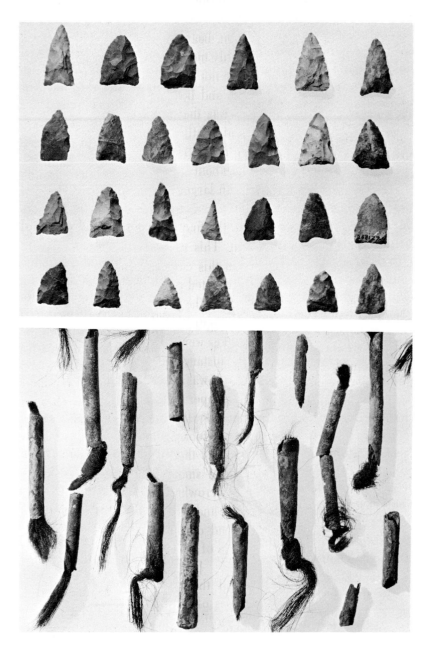

Fig. 4. — Flint arrowheads and copper hair ornaments of the Dumaw Creek Indians, about 1600. Courtesy of Chicago Natural History Museum.

wigwams, and so we can infer that the Dumaw Creek Indians possessed one of these types. And in either case their shelters were
made of poles and saplings covered with bark, skins, or woven
mats. Their village was a cluster of such dwellings, probably dome-
shaped wigwams, situated on the sandy plain about 30 feet above
the floor of a wooded V-shaped valley through which ran a small
creek. It seems doubtful to me that this creek could have been
navigable by canoe, although a canoe could be paddled to within
a mile or so of the village. To me it looks as if the Dumaw Creek
Indians were inland peoples who purposely lived away from navigable streams for the sake of protection. It is even possible that
their village was surrounded by a wooden palisade. Palisades, usually circular, were a characteristic of earlier Late Woodland villages elsewhere in Michigan and were in use by the Huron Indians
in Ontario at the time of French contact; thus the custom of building wooden fortifications was known in the region. And the particular situation of the Dumaw Creek village suggests fortification even
though direct evidence of it is lacking.

Household equipment included hearths, cooking utensils, bedding, storage facilities, tools, and utensils. Leaf-shaped, oval, and
rhomboidal knives of flint were neatly chipped on all faces and
edges (Fig. 5). Smaller and cruder knives were merely thin flakes
of flint with a finely chipped cutting edge. Scraping tools included
bipolar cores with scraping blades, thumbnail type snub-nosed
scrapers of chipped flint, and side and end scrapers made of thick
flint flakes. Sharply pointed awls probably used for sewing were
made of animal bone and wooden thorns. Ungrooved axes or hatchets of trianguloid outline (Fig. 5) were shaped from hard stone
such as diabase by pecking and grinding, then hafted through sock-
ets cut into hardwood handles. Hammers consisted of naturally
shaped cobbles of granite, gabbro, or diabase selected for their
suitability. Various sizes of woven bags, or bags made of animal
skins, served as storage containers, and possibly there were boxes
made of bark also used for that purpose. Bedding consisted of
woven mats and furs, probably beaver for the most part. There
undoubtedly were wooden ladles and bowls for the preparation
and serving of food. Possibly unworked mussel shells were used as
spoons, since several have been found with burials of Dumaw
Creek Indians. Food was cooked over hearths, some of it at least

in pottery vessels supported on stones. There were many hearths manifested by clusters of blackened and fire-cracked rocks at the Dumaw Creek village site.

Pottery was made of fired clay tempered with small particles of granitic stone. Typical vessels (Fig. 5) were broad-mouthed jars

Fig. 5. — Pipes, pots, axe, and knives of the Dumaw Creek Indians, about 1600. Courtesy of Chicago Natural History Museum.

with round bottoms, short globular bodies, a constriction between rim and body, and slightly flaring rims with scalloped or a pinched "pie crust" treatment of the lips. Vessel surfaces were covered with impressions of a fabric-wrapped or cord-wrapped paddle made while the clay was still plastic. In a number of cases the cord or fabric roughening was subsequently smoothed prior to the time of firing. This pottery was not painted but did possess coloring of tans and grays produced by the firing of the clay. Most jars ranged in height from 4 to 10 inches and the same in maximum diameter, but there were some much larger vessels also in use.

The Dumaw Creek Indians probably made their clothing of animal skins and woven fabrics. Remnants found in graves suggest that they had robes made of elk skin, beaver, bear, and raccoon. One fragment of a beaver robe made of two or more skins sewn together had curvilinear designs applied to the non-fur side with red paint. An illustration of how a Dumaw Creek Indian might have looked in such a robe is provided by Figure 6, which also shows the use of certain other articles of personal adornment: The hair, colored with powdered red ocher, was further ornamented with about sixty bright tubular beads of shining copper (see also Figs. 4 and 7). These large tubes or hair pipes were held in position by tresses of hair that had been inserted through the tubes and tied in a knot larger than the opening of any given hair pipe. Uppermost on the wearer's chest was a necklace of spheroidal beads made of white marine shells imported from the coastal waters of southeastern United States. Next there was a necklace of glistening copper beads that were small tubes made of thin sheets of hammered native copper. And in the lowermost position, suspended on a leather string, was a masklike pendant of marine shell with a weeping eye motif engraved upon it.

Other Dumaw Creek Indians wore necklaces of tubular beads made of marine shell and had their hair decorated not only with copper hair pipes but also with white beads of marine shell fastened to knotted tresses in the same manner as the hair pipes. Still another style of hair ornamentation consisted of a rectangular plaque of large copper beads worn on the back of the head in conjunction with some kind of roached headdress (Fig. 7). Additional articles of personal adornment used by the Dumaw Creek Indians were shell pendants in the form of animal or bird claws,

circular shell pendants with central perforations, a copper pendant in the form of a snake, copper tinkling cones fastened to
fringes on parts of garments or perhaps ornamented bags, and
beads made of small perforated snail shells (*Glabella* or *Prunum
apicina*) from the coastal waters of the southeastern United States.
This type of bead was found in such vast quantities in one grave
as to suggest tremendously lavish necklaces or else solid panels
of beads attached to garments or ritual paraphernalia.

Tobacco pipes of stone or fired clay were used by the Dumaw
Creek Indians. Unusual pipes were effigy forms of several kinds.
For example, there was an elbow pipe of clay with the bowl in
the form of a bird's head with a wide open mouth. A stone pipe
bowl in the shape of a half-disk with a turtle's neck and head
projecting from the upper portion (Fig. 5) was decorated with an
engraved cross design. This pipe and most of the other Dumaw
Creek styles required the addition of a wooden stem or reed inserted into a hole drilled into the base of the pipe bowl. Another
effigy pipe of ground stone (Fig. 5) was in the form of a perched
bird, probably a woodpecker or kingfisher. Most Dumaw Creek
pipes, however, were small elbow-forms or vase-shapes of stone
to which were attached wooden stems. Some vase-shaped pipes
were ornamented with engraved snakes, arrows, and geometric
forms that probably possessed symbolic meanings.

The Dumaw Creek Indians wove mats and bags of various sorts.
Neatly finished mats were made of properly prepared rushes and
spun bast fiber by using a simple plaiting technique. Rather elaborate bags were made of spun buffalo hair and leather thongs by
means of a twining technique in which the leather thongs were
twisted around the cords of buffalo hair. Small openwork bags
were made by twining with flat narrow strips of unspun bast fiber.

Burials of the Dumaw Creek Indians were somewhat elaborate.
The dead were interred in graves dug into the sandy soil on the
plain above the creek bed about a half mile from the village site.
Usually there was only one corpse to a grave pit, but sometimes
there were two. The bodies were placed in a flexed position oriented approximately along an east-west axis. In preparation for
burial the dead were dressed in all their finery and wrapped in
robes of animal skin. They were placed in the grave pits along
with tools, utensils, weapons, food, and other burial furniture

Fig. 6. — Drawing reconstructing the probable appearance of a Dumaw Creek Indian man of about 1600. Courtesy of Chicago Natural History Museum.

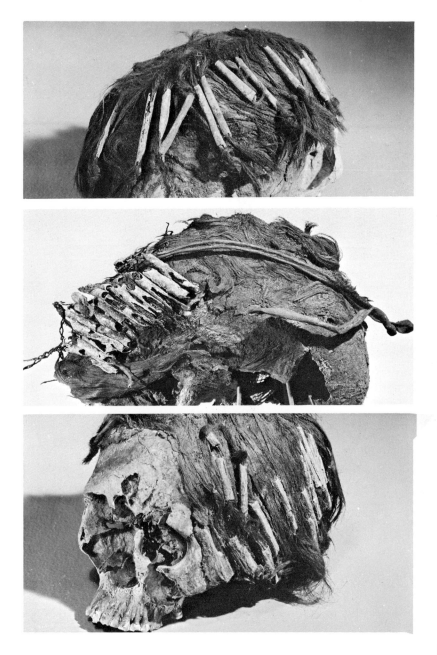

Fig. 7. — Copper hair ornaments in original position on skulls of Dumaw Creek Indians of about 1600. Courtesy of Chicago Natural History Museum.

that might be of use to them in the spirit world or on their ghostly journey to that world of the dead.

Who were the Dumaw Creek Indians who lived in western Michigan just before the dawn of the historic period? We know they were not the Iroquoian-speaking Hurons or Tobacco Hurons or Neutrals because their culture does not resemble that of those Indian nations. On a similar basis we know that they were not Winnebago or any other known Siouan tribe. Therefore the Dumaw Creek Indians must have been a part of some Algonkian-speaking nation dwelling between the Huron on the east and the Winnebago at the west. Of the Algonkian-speaking tribes we may eliminate the Shawnee and the various divisions of the Illinois who had a Mississippian type of culture. We may also eliminate the numerous groups that compose the Chippewa (also called Ojibwa) because of major differences in pottery types and pattern of settlement. This leaves the following possibilities: Miami, Menomini, Ottawa, Sauk, Fox, Kickapoo, Mascouten, and Potawatomi.

In my opinion Dumaw Creek culture was more closely adapted to a prairie type of environment than it was to a northern forest habitat where the villages were along lake shores or the banks of navigable rivers. I would therefore eliminate northern tribes such as the Menomini and Ottawa. I would also eliminate the Miami and Fox inasmuch as thus far they seem to be identified with somewhat different types of culture. It is possible that the Dumaw Creek culture is an ancestral form of Sauk, Mascouten, or even Kickapoo, but I believe it is most likely to have been Potawatomi, because the Dumaw Creek site is located in what should have been Potawatomi territory in the sixteenth and early seventeenth centuries.

As indicated previously, there are in the western Great Lakes region very few archaeologically known cultures that can be proven to have existed in the period just before the arrival of the French traders and missionaries. Dumaw Creek culture is a new addition to this brief list, but some others have been recognized adequately for the past twenty-five or so years. For instance, eastward of the Dumaw Creek Indians in the lands adjoining the south shore of Lake Huron's Georgian Bay were the village sites of the prehistoric Huron Indians, whose culture was the product of a sedentary, agricultural mode of life. There, in cleared fields in the natural prairies and openings in the southern hardwood forest, the pre-historic Hurons raised abundant crops of corn, pumpkins, beans, sunflowers (for seed), and tobacco. To a lesser degree they en-gaged in fishing and hunting in order to obtain food and raw ma-terials such as bone, antler, and skins. They also carried on trade with neighboring groups of Indians.

The archaeological evidence from Ontario indicates that the prehistoric Huron had been in existence for a considerable time when the French arrived. We are fortunate in having reasonably good ethnohistorical accounts of the Huron during their period of contact with the French, and we know quite a bit about their dispersal after they were defeated by the Iroquois in the middle of the seventeenth century (see Quimby, 1960, pp. 98–99 and 113–22).

The Hurons lived in palisaded villages, generally situated in inland positions away from navigable waterways. Their dwellings were long-houses made of frames of thick poles covered with large sheetlike shingles of bark (Fig. 8). They used wooden bows and arrows for hunting and warfare. Arrowheads of chipped flint and chert were triangular in outline, and other forms were made of antler and bone. Tools such as knives, scrapers, and drills were made of flint by chipping techniques, whereas ungrooved axes were made of hard, granular stone by pecking and grinding until the desired form was achieved.

Pottery representative of Huron culture was of several styles and was extraordinarily abundant. It was skillfully made, with a smooth and hard surface, the clay having been tempered with fine particles of grit and fired to reddish buffs or dark grays. Round-bottomed, globe-shaped jars, with wide mouths and short, flaring rims, were common. The varied embellishments included flat-topped projections, or castellations, of the rim; elliptically shaped mouths; and loop handles. Usually only the upper rim ex-teriors show decoration, consisting of an encircling band of rec-tangular or triangular areas filled with incised parallel lines. Often there was an encircling row of punctate impressions on the shoulder. Less common were open-mouth jars with round bottoms, elongated bodies, and slightly flaring, high-collared rims. Decora-tion, usually confined to the collared rim, consisted of a wide band of triangular or rectangular areas of parallel incised lines.

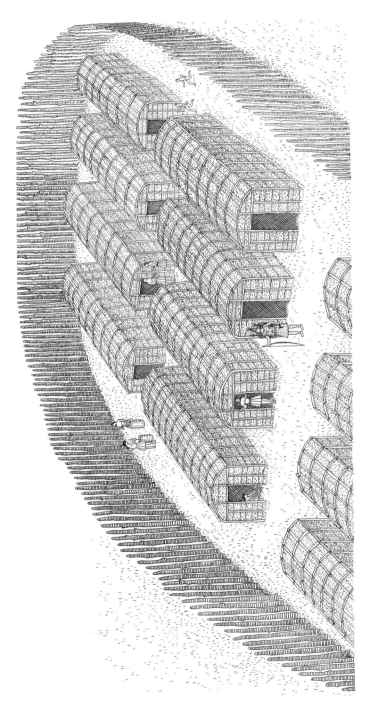

Fig. 8. — Drawing reconstructing part of a Huron village of 1615, showing long-houses and palisade. Courtesy of Chicago Natural History Museum.

Some vessels without collared rims had the same sort of decoration encircling the body of the jar.

Tobacco pipes, which were made of fired clay or stone, included both the elbow and the vase-shaped types. Among the former, trumpet-shaped bowls, barrel-shaped bowls, effigy bowls, and other elaborate shapes were quite plentiful and represent a high degree of artistry in their manufacture. The vase-shaped types were probably more plentiful and were used with added stems of bone, reed, or wood.

The prehistoric Huron as well as their later counterparts of the Early Historic period deposited their dead in a mass burial called an ossuary. At intervals of some years (eight to twelve, in later times) bodies disinterred from places of temporary burial as well as those of the recently deceased were placed in a large grave pit along with robes, tools, ornaments, weapons, food, and utensils.

At the opposite side of the western Great Lakes region was the ancient homeland of the prehistoric Winnebago Indians. This was the area just south of Green Bay, lying as the crow flies some 400 miles west of the Hurons and about 100 miles northwest of the Dumaw Creek Indians. Here, in the area around Lake Winnebago, were the ancient village sites and cemeteries from which in the present century have come the archaeological data used in the reconstructions of prehistoric Winnebago culture.

Prehistoric Winnebago culture was the product of a sedentary, agricultural mode of life. Subsistence was based on crops of corn, beans, and pumpkins supplemented by hunting, fishing, and the gathering of wild foods. The Indian bearers of this culture lived in houses framed of saplings and covered with bark or woven mats. They used wooden bows and arrows in hunting and warfare. Arrow shafts were smoothed with the aid of grooved sandstone tablets used in pairs, and finely chipped triangular arrowheads were made of flint. Other forms of arrowheads were made of bone or antler. For taking fish there were spears tipped with detachable bone points with multiple barbs on one side only, nets, lures made of shells in the form of a small fish, and bone fishhooks.

Tools included ungrooved axes of ground and polished stone; various kinds of scrapers, knives, and drills made of chipped flint; fleshing or beaming tools made of deer leg bones; mussel-shell scrapers; and bone awls. Utensils consisted of mussel-shell spoons with notched handles, mussel-shell ladles, wooden bowls and ladles, and pottery vessels. The principal pottery type of the prehistoric Winnebago has been named Lake Winnebago Trailed (see Hall, 1962, pp. 171–74). This pottery is characterized by squat, globular jars with round bottoms and rounded shoulders, a constriction between rims and upper shoulders, and more or less straight rims that slant outward at a sharp angle. Lips are squared and sometimes have shallow notches on their surfaces. Such vessels were made of clay tempered with small flakes of crushed mussel shell and fired to a proper degree of hardness, with resultant natural colors ranging in light shades of tan with reddish tints. Vessels were typically decorated only on the exterior upper body and shoulder areas. Decoration was accomplished mainly with a tool that left broad trailed lines with well-defined margins or elongated and rectangular punctations when it was punched into the still plastic clay before it had dried. The simplest designs were those in which vertical lines were repeated in a band around the body, but more common were areas of vertical lines alternated with or placed beneath zones of horizontal lines (see Hall, 1962, Plates 74–75). Often a line of punctate impressions encircled the neck of the vessel just below the rim. Jars of this type ranged from about 4 to 16 inches in maximum diameter.

Ornaments of the prehistoric Winnebago Indians included pendants of sheet copper, stone, or shell; engraved tubes of bird bones; and beads of bone, shell, or thin sheet copper rolled into tubes. Tobacco pipes were made of polished stone, frequently of catlinite, and were of a very characteristic disk-shaped variety. The dead were buried in individual grave pits, usually in an extended position but sometimes in a flexed position. Food, tools, utensils, weapons, and ornaments were placed with the deceased in their graves so that they would have the use of them on their journey to the world of the dead.

Like prehistoric Winnebago, to which it is closely related, the Blue Island culture was the product of gardening Indians who were more or less sedentary. They tilled their fields with hoes made of mussel shells or shoulder blades of elk and other large animals, and probably raised corn, pumpkins, beans, and tobacco, supplementing their vegetal diet by hunting, fishing, and the gathering of wild food. White-tailed deer, beaver, muskrat, and raccoon were among animals frequently taken. To a lesser degree elk, squirrel, wolf, black bear, otter, skunk, mink, mountain lion, many kinds of birds, reptiles, and fish were utilized for food and raw materials. Shellfish, snails, and vegetal products were also collected for food and other purposes. These Indians lived in rectangular or elongated houses made of upright saplings set into the ground, probably bent over and tied at the top, reinforced by lateral poles on the roof and sides, and covered most likely with woven mats. Such houses ranged in size from 10 by 25 feet to 15 by 55 feet.

Village sites and cemeteries associated with the Blue Island culture occur only in southeastern Cook County, near Chicago, an area which in the prehistoric period was prairie land, devoid of trees except in stream valleys and swamps. Of all the village or cemetery sites manifesting the Blue Island culture, the most spectacular was the Anker site (see Bluhm and Liss, 1961, pp. 89–137). It was unusual in many ways. The amount and quality of the burial furniture in the cemetery suggested that these people must have been an extraordinarily wealthy group. Moreover the presence of objects from the high cultural areas of the central Mississippi Valley and elsewhere suggests that the Anker site may have been an important trading center at the southern periphery of the western Great Lakes. And finally, the large structure, 13 by 55 feet, may represent a ceremonial building which, taken with the wealth of domestic and imported goods in the graves, could be considered indicative of an important ceremonial center for the Indians representative of the Blue Island culture.

The Anker site was located on the north side of the Little Calumet River, south of Chicago in Thornton Township of Cook County, Illinois. At the time of occupancy the site was near a stand of deciduous trees on the prairie, beside a clear-running stream. In the burial grounds at the edge of the village there were sixty or more graves. At least half of the cemetery population had been buried in an extended position on their backs in oval pits dug into the yellow clay beneath the topsoil. Other burials consisted of bundles of bones, probably the remains of individuals moved from other repositories of the dead and interred in this cemetery. Most of the extended burials were accompanied by an abundance of grave goods: tools, utensils, weapons, ornaments, and ceremonial objects.

A mink skull and wildcat and otter skulls with inlaid eyes of sheet copper found with burials were undoubtedly the remains of sacred medicine bundles of types used in the region until recent times. Other ritual paraphernalia found with the dead included wolf jaws, a loon beak wrapped in sheet copper, and a human long bone with notches cut into it.

Tools, weapons, and ornaments from the Anker site were similar to those from the Dumaw Creek site. There were triangular arrowheads; leaf-shaped, biface knives; ovoid scrapers; knives made of sharpened flakes; and drills, all made of chipped flint. Ungrooved axes were made of ground and polished diorite, arrow shaft smoothers were grooved tablets made of sandstone, and hammers were selected from waterworn pebbles. Awls, matting needles, arrowheads, beaming tools, arrow shaft straighteners, and flaking tools were made of bone and antler. Beaver incisors were used as chisels. There were ear ornaments made of wood covered with a layer of hammered copper, tubular beads of sheet copper, copper hair pipes, tinkling cones of sheet copper, finger rings of copper, C-shaped bracelets of copper, and snake effigy pendants made of copper. An unusual ornament was a small piece of antler carved in the form of a perched bird resting on a separate pedestal, also of carved antler. Copper tinkling cones found beneath it were originally fastened to perforations in the bird's tail. Other ornaments were various styles of beads made of imported marine shell, circular pendants of marine shell, a T-shaped ear ornament of marine shell and masklike gorgets of marine shell with modeled nose and engraved "weeping eye" design beneath drilled and engraved eyes.

Utensils at the Anker site consisted of notched mussel-shell spoons and distinctive ceramics characteristic of the Blue Island culture of which this site is a spectacular manifestation. Pottery was made of shell-tempered clay fired to a gray color. Decoration applied before firing, while the clay was still plastic, consisted of wide trailed lines or narrow incised lines arranged in vertical or slanting groups in a wide band around the shoulder areas of globular jars. Sometimes rows of punctate impressions were included. Such jars, ranging in diameter from 4 to 20 inches, had round bottoms, rounded shoulders terminating in a slight constriction at the base of short, slightly flaring rims, and broad orifices. Vessel lips often were notched in various ways, but a scalloped appearance produced by fingers was not uncommon. Loop handles on the rim in pairs or in fours were also in common use, probably to suspend these jars over a fire. Pottery like that in common use at the Anker site is more closely related to the pottery of the prehistoric Winnebago than it is to the other cultural groups mentioned in this chapter.

Tobacco pipes were made of stone, and all required the addition of a stem of wood or bone. There were elbow pipes, a vase-shaped pipe, a block-shaped pipe, and a pipe shaped like an ungrooved axe head, upon both sides of which were engraved crude figures of bison, some of which had lines or conventionalized arrows connecting the mouth with the heart or the heart area — a motif known in many American Indian tribes of later times. Disk pipes like those of the prehistoric Winnebago had flat, horizontal disks mounted on tapered platforms. The bowl of the pipe was in the disk and the stem hole was in the platform. One of the disk pipes from the Anker site had a hollow stem made of human bone. There was one pipe in the shape of a truncated cone, another in the form of a bear's head, and a rather striking effigy pipe carved in the form of a human head with pursed lips, hollow eyes, puffed-out cheeks, and enlongated earlobes which have been perforated. The style of this pipe suggests Iroquoian influences from the east.

The Anker and some other sites manifesting Blue Island culture antedate the arrival of European culture in the region. The tribal affiliation of Blue Island culture is not known, but upon the basis of close similarities with prehistoric Winnebago and its relatives, I would suspect that Blue Island culture manifests a Siouan group related to the Winnebago in the western Great Lakes region and to other Siouan groups in the upper Mississippi Valley. It is possible, however, that Blue Island culture represents some ancient group of Miami Indians who were strongly influenced by Siouan peoples such as the prehistoric Winnebago. The similarities between the Anker site and the Dumaw Creek site some 200 miles to the north suggest cultural connections probably in the category of trading relationships. Triangular arrowheads and shell-tempered pottery like some of that typical of Blue Island culture have been found as far north as the junction of the Thornapple and Grand rivers in Kent County, Michigan, within 75 miles of the Dumaw Creek site.

Less than 200 miles north of the Dumaw Creek site, on Bois Blanc Island near the Straits of Mackinac, there is a stratified Late Woodland site that was excavated by the University of Michigan. The uppermost level of this site contains materials representative of an Indian occupancy probably of a period not long antedating the arrival of the French in the western Great Lakes region (see McPherron, 1963, p. 575). Pottery associated with the uppermost level is somewhat similar to that of the Dumaw Creek Indians. This particular pottery from Bois Blanc Island is characterized by wide-mouth jars of fired clay tempered with small particles of rock. Outflaring rims, generally smooth, have lips that have been finger-fluted, scalloped, or pinched like those of Dumaw Creek vessels and like those of one of the pottery types found at a Fox Indian site of a later period in Wisconsin (see Chap. 9). Other cultural traits from the uppermost level of this site were also similar to some of those found at Dumaw Creek and at the Fox Indian site in Wisconsin. Upon this basis I would conclude that there was a very late prehistoric village of some Algonkian-speaking Indians, probably Sauk or Potawatomi, possibly Fox, Mascouten, or Kickapoo, advantageously situated on Bois Blanc Island so as to make use of the excellent fishing grounds in the adjacent shallows.

Lower levels of this same site (McPherron, 1963, pp. 573–74) and various sites on the north shore of Lake Michigan (see Binford and Quimby, 1963, pp. 282–85) that belong to the Late Woodland period (A.D. 800 to 1600) manifest a culture that is quite different from those I have described previously in this chapter. Villages were located along the shores of the Great Lakes, in areas suitable for safe launchings or landings of birchbark canoes, or were similarly situated along large inland lakes and the banks of navigable rivers near their mouths. In each instance the village was placed near a major fishing area where there was an abundance of very large fish such as sturgeon, lake trout, or whitefish. But villages were not placed adjacent to bad or dangerous canoe landings even in areas of good fishing grounds. Thus the most important single criterion of locality for the establishment of a village was the availability of a good place for the landing of birchbark canoes. I feel certain, however, that if good fishing areas had not been more abundant than good village sites some other major principle of locality would have been established.

The abundance of fish and the means to catch them and utilize them for food were the foundation of village life in the northern Great Lakes, just as agriculture was the basis of village life in the southern part of the region. These northern villages were occupied only in the spring and summer months, probably by local exogamous kindreds or patrilineal totemic groups (see Hickerson, 1962, Chaps. 5 and 6) which of necessity separated into small family units during the winter months and subsisted by hunting in areas far removed from the summer villages.

The Late Woodland culture manifested by the archaeological remains of the sites of these summer villages in the northern part of the region was the product of essentially a fishing and hunting economy. Fish were taken in weirs and nets, by bone fishhook and line, and by spears tipped with unilaterally barbed harpoon heads made of bone or antler. Wooden bows and arrows were used for hunting. The arrows were tipped with points of bone, antler, or chipped flint. The flint arrowheads were either triangular like those from Dumaw Creek or were stemmed and notched forms. Other weapons and tools of flint included a few kinds of knives and various scrapers, one type of which was produced by the bipolar flint-knapping technique (see Binford and Quimby, 1963).

Pottery was of several styles which were different from the kinds previously described in this chapter. In a general comparison this different pottery can be said to consist of relatively long-bodied jars with rather broad mouths and subconoidal bases. It was made of clay mixed with particles of crushed stone, and vessel surfaces were uniformly roughened by impressions of a fabric or cord-wrapped paddle. One style was characterized by collars and castellations of the rim and the use of push and pull incising for a technique of decoration. The recognizable characteristics of another style were outflaring rims with thickened lips and techniques of decoration consisting of impressing a cord-wrapped stick or an edged tool wrapped with cord to produce simple geometric patterns on the lip and both the exterior and the interior of the rims. Sometimes simple punctates were included in the ornamentation. Another style of this pottery was characterized by simple patterns of horizontal lines on the rim exterior produced by impressing with cords or with a tool that makes a pseudo-cord impression. Simple punctate impressions widely spaced were used as a border element in these patterns, and surfaces of lip thickenings were ornamented with closely spaced cord or pseudo-cord impressions. Still another style of pottery, undecorated except for notched lips, was readily recognizable because the exterior was covered by impressions of a fabric. A similar and closely related style was characterized by impressions of a cord-wrapped paddle applied to the exterior, and the only decoration was a notched lip or, less frequently, cord-wrapped stick impressions on the interior of the rim.

Tools and weapons of bone and antler included awls, flakers, flat matting needles, unilaterally barbed harpoon heads for fish spears, conical arrowheads, and flat arrowheads of several shapes. Ungrooved axes were made of hard granular stone and were like those from the Dumaw Creek site. Copper implements included small awls and tanged knives shaped somewhat like a butter knife. Tobacco pipes usually were of elbow type, made of fired clay, with stems long enough so they could be smoked without the addition of a wooden stem piece. Ornaments included tubular copper beads and large tinkling cones of copper.

Manifestations of this particular grouping of Late Woodland cultures are found not only along the shores of northern Lake Michigan and northern Lake Huron but also along the shores of Lake Superior (see Wright, 1963, pp. 5–6) Almost certainly some of these northern sites were the products of the diverse proto-Chippewa groups, but whether they all were of this category is not yet known.

The Indian cultures that have been described in this chapter are known only from the remains they left behind them, an unintentional record, parts of which can be read by archaeologists. Yet it was either the Indians manifesting these cultures or the immediate descendants of these Indians who witnessed the coming of the Europeans and the beginning of the historic period. And these were the kinds of cultures seen by the Europeans at the times of their first contacts with the Indians of the western Great Lakes region, before the changes caused by acculturation had taken place.

The cultural change produced by contact with Europeans was

slow at first, but as time went on, the change became progressively more rapid until finally there was hardly any resemblance between what had been and what was. The power of Europe, specifically that of France, penetrated into the interior of North America, into the western Great Lakes region. That power is best symbolized for me by the arrival of an armed French merchant ship in Lake Huron and Lake Michigan. This was La Salle's sailing vessel, the *Griffin*, an account of which is presented in the next chapter.

REFERENCES

Binford and Quimby, 1963; Bluhm and Fenner, 1961; Bluhm and Liss, 1961; Hall, 1962; Hickerson, 1962; McPherron, 1963; Quimby, 1961, and field notes; Wright, 1963.

CHAPTER 4

THE FIRST EUROPEAN TRADE SHIP
ON THE WESTERN GREAT LAKES

By the end of the seventeenth century French explorers, traders, and missionaries had spread their efforts into all parts of the western Great Lakes region. Fortunes could be made in the fur trade, and there were great numbers of heathens potentially available for conversion to Christianity. One of the most interesting trading ventures of the period was that of René-Robert Cavelier, Sieur de la Salle, who in 1679 had built for him a sailing ship designed to carry cargoes of trade goods to the Indians of the western or upper Great Lakes and to return laden with large quantities of furs to the eastern or lower Great Lakes.

Although the venture miscarried and consequently failed to establish a pattern of shipping in the fur trade, it is worth recounting here in some detail. The story of the *Griffin* is intriguing as an unsolved mystery and as a unique vignette in the annals of the historic period in the Great Lakes region. La Salle's vessel was the first European trade ship to sail on Lake Huron and Lake Michigan. Within one year — 1679 — she was built, rigged, and sailed to an unknown destination from which she departed and subsequently disappeared, apparently for all time. What the *Griffin* looked like, her size, where she went, and what happened to her are not known with certainty to this day. However, in this chapter I intend to try to answer these questions by means of ethnohistorical analysis and the kinds of insights used by archaeologists for cultural and historical reconstructions.

The *Griffin* often has been depicted as a large three-masted ship, the typical man-of-war and freighter of the seventeenth century. Such a ship shown in Lake Michigan and also in Lake Huron on the Franquelin map of 1688 (see Tucker, 1942, Plate 11-B) is probably meant to represent the *Griffin*. Some museum exhibits and book illustrations also portray the *Griffin* as a large seventeenth-century freighter with three masts and elaborate rigging. In reality La Salle's vessel was a much more modest boat and not at all like the magnificent freighters or men-of-war that usually have been the basis for pictorial reconstructions of the *Griffin*.

Father Louis Hennepin, the Recollect missionary quoted in Chapter 1, witnessed the building of the *Griffin* and was a passenger on the vessel during part of the voyage. From his written account of it and from various other sources of information it has been possible to find out in a general way what kind of vessel the *Griffin* really was and where she sailed to in the upper Great Lakes.

The Building of the Griffin

The *Griffin* was built in the late winter and the spring of 1679, above Niagara Falls, probably at the mouth of Cayuga Creek. Of the building of this vessel Father Hennepin (1698, Chap. 16, pp. 62–65) wrote:

On the 22d of the said Month [January], we went two leagues above the great Fall of Niagara, where we made a Dock for building the Ship we wanted for our Voyage. This was the most convenient place we could pitch upon, being upon a River which falls into the Streight between the Lake Erie and the great Fall of Niagara. The 26th [January], the Keel of the Ship and some other Pieces being ready, Mr. la Salle sent the Master-Carpenter to desire me to drive in the first Pin; but my Profession obliging me to decline that Honour, he did it himself, and promis'd Ten Louis d'Or, to encourage the Carpenter and further the Work.

. . . our Men continued with great application to build our Ship; for the Iroquois who were left behind, being but a small number, were not so insolent as before, tho' they came now and then to our Dock, and expressed some Discontent at what we were doing. One of them in particular, feigning himself drunk, attempted to kill our Smith, but was vigorously repuls'd by him with a red-hot Iron-barr, which, together with the Reprimand he receiv'd from me, oblig'd him to be gone. Some few Days after, a Savage Woman gave us notice that the [Indians] had resolv'd to burn our Ship in the Dock, and had certainly done it, had we not been always on our guard.

These frequent alarms from the Natives, together with the Fears we were in of wanting Provisions, . . . were a great Discouragement to our Carpenters, whom, on the other hand, a Villain amongst us endeavour'd to seduce: That pitiful Fellow had several times attempted to run away from us into New-York, and would have likely perverted our Carpenters, had I not confirm'd them in their Good Resolution. . . .

The two Savages we had taken into our Service, went all this while a Hunting, and supply'd us with Wild-Goats [deer] and other Beasts for our subsistence; which encourag'd our Workmen to go on with their Work more briskly than before, insomuch that in a short time our Ship was in a readiness to be launch'd; which we did, after having Bless'd the same according to the use of the Romish Church. We made all the haste we could to get it a-float, tho' not altogether finish'd to prevent the Designs of the Natives, who had resolv'd to burn it.

The Ship was call'd the Griffin, alluding to the Arms of Count Frontenac, which have two Griffins for Supporters; and besides, M. la Salle us'd to say of this Ship, while yet up-on the Stocks, That he would make the Griffin fly above the Ravens. We fir'd three Guns, and sung Te Deum, which was attended with loud Acclamations of Joy; of which those of the Iroquois who were accidently [sic] present at this Ceremony, were also Partakers; for we gave them some Brandy to drink, as well as to our Men, who immediately quitted their Cabins of Rinds of Trees, and hang'd their Hammocks under the Deck of the Ship, there to lie with more security than a-shoar. We did the like, insomuch that the very same Day we were all on board and thereby out of the reach of the Insults of the Savages.

The Iroquois being return'd from Hunting Beavers, were mightily surpriz'd to see our Ship a-float, and call'd us Otkon, that is in their Language, Most penetrating Wits: For they could not apprehend how in so short a time we had been able to build so great a Ship, tho' it was but [45 or] 60 Tuns. It might have been indeed call'd a moving Fortress for all the Savages inhabiting the Banks of those Lakes and Rivers I have mention'd, for five hundred Leagues together, were fill'd with Fear as well as Admiration when they saw it.

A master carpenter, a blacksmith, and fewer than ten other carpenters and workmen built and launched the *Griffin* in the period between January 22 and May 27, 1679. When one considers that the wood came from trees felled near-by and that of the ship's timbers and planking had to be cut and shaped *in situ*, then fitted into place and fastened, it does not seem possible that so few men could have built a ship of any great size in a period of approximately four months.

THE SIZE OF THE GRIFFIN

Although there are no direct statements concerning the dimensions of the *Griffin* there are statements of her burden or cargo capacity. Hennepin (1698, Chap. 16, p. 66) says the *Griffin* "was but 60 Tuns" burden. In earlier editions of his work he said the ship was about 45 tons burden (see Parkman, 1894, p. 135). It is thus a fair conclusion that the *Griffin* was of 45 to 60 tons burden. In the seventeenth and eighteenth centuries, and even now in some ·cases, such a ton was not a unit of weight but a unit of space, specifically 40 cubic feet, which can be encompassed in a block 4 feet long, 5 feet wide, and 2 feet deep. If the *Griffin* was of 60 tons burden, she had a capacity of 2,400 cubic feet (60×40), which is the equivalent of a box 40 feet long, 10 feet wide, and 6 feet deep. If the *Griffin* was of 45 tons burden, she had a capacity of 1,800 cubic feet (45×40), which is the equivalent of a box 30 feet long, 10 feet wide, and 6 feet deep.

The formula for computing tonnage in Colonial times, according to Samuel Eliot Morison (1925, p. 14), was the length of the ship on deck, minus three-fifths of the greatest breadth, multiplied by the greatest breadth, multiplied by the depth of the hold, divided by 95. With this formula, the tonnage of the *Griffin,* and some additional clues, one can approximate the probable dimensions of the vessel.

One of these additional clues concerns the draught (depth below water line) of the *Griffin.* On August 24, 1679, the *Griffin* was in Lake Huron, according to Hennepin (1698, Chap. 21, p. 83), "becalm'd between some Islands, where we found but two Fathoms Water, which oblig'd us to make an easie sail part of the Night." Thus the *Griffin* could navigate satisfactorily though cautiously in 12 feet of water. To do this the ship would have had to have a draught of much less than 12 feet. Even a draught of 6 feet would require extreme caution in sailing through uncharted waters of 2 fathoms. Some additional evidence that the *Griffin* was of no great draught is suggested by the fact that in the autumn of 1679, when La Salle was still ignorant of the loss of his vessel, he was expecting the *Griffin* to arrive at an anchorage in the St. Joseph River near its mouth. In the days before man-made breakwaters and dredging of channels, all rivers such as the St. Joseph had shoals and sand bars beneath their waters where they entered Lake Michigan. The depth at the entrance to the St. Joseph River probably was not more than 6 feet in 1679, and possibly less than that. For instance, the Grand River, flowing into Lake Michigan 60 miles to the north, was more than twice the size of the St. Joseph River, yet the Grand River had only 12 feet of water over the sand bar at its entrance, according to the log book of the British sloop *Felicity*, which entered the river on October 31, 1779. It seems unreasonable to suppose that the entrance to the St. Joseph River, even a hundred years earlier, could have in any way matched the depth at the mouth of the Grand River.

Another clue involves proportions of seventeenth-century vessels, which were more box-like than nineteenth-century sailing ships. For instance, it is stated in "A Treatise on Shipbuilding, 1620–1625" (see Glasgow, 1964, p. 179) that in building ships, "the depth must never be greater than half the breadth nor less [than] one-third and the length never less than double nor more than treble the breadth." Writing at a somewhat earlier date (*circa* 1600), William Borough stated that "Merchant ships for most profit" should be built so as "to have the length of the keel double the breadth amidship and the depth in hold half that breadth" (Glasgow, 1964, p. 179). On this basis a vessel with a keel 40 feet long would have had a breadth amidship of 20 feet and a depth of hold of 10 feet. This would have been a vessel of at least 58 tons, and about the maximum size of the *Griffin*.

Another one of William Borough's ideal vessel types was "Shipping for merchandise likewise very serviceable for all purposes." Such shipping should be constructed so as to have the "length of the keel two or two and a quarter that of the beam" and "depth of hold eleven twenty-fourths that of beam" (Glasgow, 1964, p. 179). If the *Griffin* had been built according to these specifications and was of 47 or 48 tons burden, she would have been about 40.5 feet long and 18 feet wide with a hold 8.5 feet deep. But whatever system of proportions was used in the building of the *Griffin*, she probably was designed for cargo capacity rather than speed and maneuverability. Moreover, she probably was of 45 tons burden rather than 60 tons. In either case, the *Griffin* was a small vessel somewhat similar to the British ships of the same period, the *Nonesuch* and the *Eaglet*. The *Eaglet*, of the British South Seas Fleet, was 40 feet long and 16 feet wide. The *Nonesuch*, which sailed from England to Hudson's Bay and back again in 1668–69, had a keel 36 feet long, a beam of 15 feet, and was of 43 tons burden.

The available evidence indicates to me that the *Griffin* was a small vessel, probably of 45 tons burden and between 35 and 45 feet in length. It seems likely that her greatest width was between 16 and 20 feet and her depth of hold was 7.5 to 10 feet. She probably had a draught of 4 or 5 feet.

THE RIGGING OF THE GRIFFIN

The anchors, cables, ropes, sails, rigging, and other fittings for the *Griffin* were shipped from Fort Frontenac by sailing vessels to the head of Lake Ontario, then carried on foot to the temporary shipyard above Niagara Falls. Father Hennepin noted that the *Griffin* was completely finished and rigged by July 4 of 1679 (Hennepin, 1698, Chap. 18, p. 73).

Father Hennepin wrote very little about the rigging of the *Griffin*. He mentions a vessel rigged as a brigantine (his use of the term "bark" referred to a small vessel and not a type of rig) on Lake Ontario and should have said so had the *Griffin* been thus rigged. Hennepin did say (1698, Chap. 18, p. 73) of the *Griffin* that she was "well Rigg'd, and ready fitted out with all the Necessaries for Sailing." With reference to a storm on Lake Huron, Hennepin (1698, Chap. 21, p. 84) wrote: ". . . we brought down our Main Yards and Top-Mast, and let the Ship drive to the Mercy of the Wind." When the storm was over, ". . . we hoisted up our Sail. . . ." With these few simple but positive statements it is possible to make some observations about the rigging of the *Griffin*.

The mention of a "Top-Mast" and "Main Yards" suggests that the *Griffin* was not rigged as a ketch. The ketch of this period was rigged with lateen sails and did not need topmasts. Moreover, the ketch rig would have had only one main yard (set diagonally), and Hennepin's use of "Yards" implies that there was more than one yard on the mainmast. Had the *Griffin* been rigged as a ship or a

brig there would have been more than one topmast to bring down
during a storm such as he describes. Also in such an instance there
would have been only one main yard and a number of other yards
to bring down. And, finally, ship or brig or brigantine rigging unless unusually modified would have been too complicated for a
pilot and five men to handle on the return voyage to Niagara. (This
was the number dispatched by La Salle, according to Hennepin.)

The only direct evidence from Hennepin's account of it suggests
that the *Griffin* had a main mast, a main topmast, and two yards
for square sails that were set on this compound mast. In short, the
driving sails of the *Griffin* were on the mainmast and by implica-
tion any other sails used must have been very small and set on a
mast or masts that could have been removed from the deck by one
or two persons and did not require shrouds for their support. Such
small sails, if present, were used for balance and ease of steering.
The only driving sails were on the mainmast.

That such rigging was known in the seventeenth century is dem-
onstrated by the pictorial embellishments on the Franquelin map
of 1689 (see Griffin, 1943, map 10). On that map in the area of
the Gulf of Mexico there are pictured two small sailing vessels 30
to 40 feet long, each with a large mainmast and a small foremast
stepped close to the bow and tilted forward. The large driving
sails, two of them, both square in outline, and each with its own
yard, are set on the mainmast. A small sail, as much for balance
as drive, is set on the short foremast. This style of rigging would
correlate perfectly with Father Hennepin's statements about the
rigging on the *Griffin* and how she was handled during the storm
on Lake Huron in late August of 1679.

It is possible that the *Griffin* had also a small lateen (triangular) sail, primarily for balance, set on a short mizzenmast
directly behind the mainmast, somewhat like an eighteenth-
century snow; or it is possible that the *Griffin* was rigged only
with a conventional mizzen sail and mainsails. Whatever the case,
it seems most probable that the mainmast with its topmast was
the only important mast on the *Griffin* and that the mainsail and
main topsail were the most important sails. All other sails and
masts were small and could be handled completely from the deck
of the *Griffin*.

The Appearance of the Griffin

The *Griffin*, then, let us assume, was a sailing vessel between 35 and 40 feet in length and 45 tons burden, rigged with a mainmast, main topmast, mainsail and topsail and possibly a small foresail set on a stumpy foremast. She was heavily built, a floating fortress as she was called by Father Hennepin and some of the Indians who saw her. According to Hennepin (1698, Chap. 18, p. 73), "She carry'd Five small Guns [cannon], two whereof were Brass, and three Harquebrize a-crock [swivel guns for rampart defense]. The Beak-head [a beak-like projection of the bow fastened to the stem and supported by the main knee] was adorn'd with a Flying Griffin, and an Eagle above it; and the rest of the ship had the same Ornaments as Men of War used to have." There were at

Fig. 9. — Reconstructions of the *Griffin*, built in 1679. Courtesy of Chicago Natural History Museum.

least two anchors so big, according to Hennepin (1698, Chap. 18, p. 75) "that four Men had much ado to carry one." Although Hennepin did not mention it, the *Griffin* probably carried one or more birchbark canoes in place of longboats for passage between ship and shore. In Figure 9 there are presented four drawings of the *Griffin* based on the factual statements and inferences that have been presented here.

THE VOYAGE OF THE GRIFFIN

The ship with provisions, tools, ammunition, and commodities for trade left its anchorage near the Niagara River on August 7, 1679. On board were Father Hennepin, La Salle, Henri de Tonti (his lieutenant), the pilot, and thirty other men, including two missionaries. By modern standards the *Griffin* might seem somewhat crowded, but it is elsewhere on record that the *Eaglet*, a ship of the same dimensions I have attributed to the *Griffin*, carried a war complement of thirty-five men on much longer voyages than that of La Salle's ship.

The *Griffin* reached the mouth of the Detroit River on August 10, 1679. It took four days of sailing to run the length of Lake Erie, a distance of about 240 miles. On this leg of the voyage the longest daily run mentioned by Hennepin was 45 leagues (124.38 miles).

Although Hennepin's statements are not clear on the matter, it looks as if the *Griffin* passed up the Detroit River through Lake St. Clair and up the St. Clair River between August 11 and August 21. On August 22, 1679 (see Hennepin, 1698, Chap. 21, pp. 83–84), the *Griffin* began the Lake Huron leg of her voyage and completed it on August 27, a period of six days in which she sailed more than 240 miles. The vessel anchored in a bay at Michilimackinac (which would be East Moran Bay at present-day St. Ignace, Michigan) in "six Fathoms Water upon a slimy white Bottom." In 36 feet of water the *Griffin* was either some distance from the shore or else closer to the shore off Graham Point at the southeast extremity of the bay. Hennepin's observation about the lake bottom in this area is correct. At Michilimackinac in 1679 there was a Huron village, an Ottawa village, a Jesuit mission, and an establishment of Frenchmen who traded with the Indians of the region.

On September 2, 1679, the *Griffin* left Michilimackinac and, according to Father Hennepin (1698, Chap. 22, p. 88),

sailed into the Lake of the Illinois [Lake Michigan]; and came to an Island just at the Mouth of the Bay of the Pauns [Green Bay], lying about forty Leagues [110.56 miles] from Missilimakinak [Michilimackinac, or St. Ignace]: It is inhabit'd by some Savages of the Nation call'd Poutoua-tamis, with whom some of the Men M. la Salle had sent the Year before had barter'd a great quantity of Furrs [*sic*] and Skins.

Hennepin wrote very little about this island, but he went on to say (1698, Chap. 22, p. 89):

Our Ship was riding in the Bay, about thirty Paces [75 feet] from the furthermost Point of the Land, upon a pretty good Anchorage, where we rode safely, notwithstanding a violent Storm which lasted four Days. [The chief of the Potawatomis] seeing our Ship toss'd up by the Waves, and not knowing it was able to resist, ventur'd himself in his little Canow, and came to our assistance. He had the good Luck to get safe on board.

ANALYSIS OF THE VOYAGE

The first legs or segments of the voyage of the *Griffin* seem reasonably clear and are not particularly interesting from my point of view except for details concerning the vessel itself and how it sailed under different conditions, the pattern of the navigation of La Salle's pilot, and what distances were traversed in a given time. Except at Michilimackinac there were no Indian tribes encountered on the first portions of the voyage of the *Griffin*. The last leg of the upbound journey and the events immediately following are the most uncertain and the most interesting to me at this time.

In early September of 1679, as stated just above, the *Griffin* left Michilimackinac on Lake Huron and sailed westward through the Straits of Mackinac across northern Lake Michigan for about 40 leagues, or 110 miles, to an island lying just at the opening into Green Bay and inhabited by Potawatomi Indians. There are seven islands between Lake Michigan and Green Bay, any one of which might be considered to be about 40 leagues from Michilimackinac depending upon the course one sailed to reach them (see Charts 7 and 702, War Department, Corps of Engineers, *Survey of the Northern and Northwestern Lakes*, U.S. Lake Survey Office). From north to south, these islands are Summer, Poverty, St. Martin, Rock, Washington, Detroit, and Plum. It would be of great archaeological and historical interest to know which of these islands was inhabited by Potawatomi Indians and was visited by the *Griffin* in September of 1679.

The pilot of the *Griffin*, in the absence of marine charts and modern navigation aids, should have coasted the north shore of Lake Michigan to reach Green Bay. Any available information the pilot could have had in 1679 would have come from those who made the trip by canoe and any course other than one that kept the coast in view was loaded with potential dangers in terms of passages and landfalls at the Green Bay end of the voyage. Moreover, in the earlier trip through Lakes Erie and Huron, the pilot had manifested a pattern of following the shore line. He also had established the pattern of sounding (measuring the depth of the water) probably at frequent intervals. In brief, what little evidence does exist suggests that the pilot would have sailed a course parallel to but considerably offshore of the established canoe route from Michilimackinac to Green Bay. This was essentially the same procedure I witnessed in 1939 when the pilot of an auxiliary ketch traveling the then uncharted waters of the east coast of Hudson's Bay followed a course that kept the shore in sight, did not sail at night, and made frequent soundings. This course was parallel to but outside of the course I had previously taken through the same area by canoe. If in 1679 the pilot of the *Griffin* followed the north shore of Lake Michigan for about 40 leagues, he would have come to Summer Island in Delta County, Michigan.

Summer Island is the first island "lying just at the mouth" of Green Bay, if one is approaching from the north. Summer Island is the second largest of the seven islands previously mentioned. At its northeast extremity there is a bay that affords good anchorage for a ship the size or even twice the size of the *Griffin*. Moreover, in this bay it is possible to anchor within "thirty paces" (75 feet) of the "furthermost point of the land"; in fact, I have done it in a 60-foot sailing vessel with a draught of 8 feet. If the *Griffin* had been anchored in this bay in 1679, the storm that tossed her for four days must have come from the northeast, because this anchorage is protected from all other directions by land, shoals, and the mainland. Adjoining this bay there is an Indian village site, on a more or less level sandy area. Artifacts collected from this site indicate occupancies representing Middle Woodland,

Late Woodland, Upper Mississippi, and perhaps historic cultures (Quimby, field notes, 1959). Summer Island could have been the Green Bay terminus of the voyage of the *Griffin*, and it is my first choice in this reconstruction of history.

Of the six remaining islands previously mentioned as possibilities, I would reject Poverty, St. Martin, Detroit, and Plum because they provide no anchorage in a bay within 75 feet of a point of land. Furthermore, these islands are either too swampy or rocky or barren. But Rock and Washington islands are possibilities even though they are more than 40 leagues from Michilimackinac. Heretofore Washington Island (Door County, Wisconsin) has been considered to be the island that the *Griffin* sailed to in Green Bay. It is the largest island in Green Bay. On its northwest end there is a beautiful narrow bay open to the north. Although there is no "furthermost point of the land" a ship could anchor anywhere in this bay within 75 feet of land and still be in water 30 to 80 feet deep. At the northwest entrance to this harbor there are white stone cliffs more than 100 feet high. The shore line is composed of cliffs, rocks, or boulder and cobble beaches. About one-half mile west of this harbor there is an Indian village site and cemetery that has produced trade materials indicative of some time between 1670 and 1760.

Although Washington Harbor on Washington Island would have been a good anchorage for the *Griffin*, it does not fit Father Hennepin's limited observations as well as does the bay on Summer Island. Furthermore, any storm that would have "tossed" the *Griffin* in Washington Harbor would have come from a northern quadrant. Under such conditions (field observations, 1958) huge waves crash over the rocky shores of this bay and it would seem virtually impossible for the Potawatomi chief to have launched a canoe without pounding out its bottom. Other bays and harbors on Washington Island, prior to dredging in modern times, would not have provided suitable anchorage for the *Griffin*. However, either side of a sandy hook off the southwest end of Rock Island would fulfill the requirements of Father Hennepin's observations and at the same time would provide a place from which a canoe might be launched in a storm. But Rock Island almost connects with Washington Island, and I would have expected Father Hennepin to make some further observation about two islands in such close proximity. Thus after considering all seven of the islands lying at the opening from Lake Michigan into Green Bay, I favor Summer Island. There is, however, some additional evidence in favor of this choice and against the other islands.

On September 18, 1679, La Salle and his men parted company with the *Griffin*, which, manned by a small crew, set sail for Niagara to deliver her cargo of furs, after which she was expected to return to the upper lakes and rejoin La Salle in the St. Joseph River of southwest Michigan. When the four canoes carrying Hennepin, La Salle, and twelve of his men left the Island of the Potawatomis, on September 19, to begin a trip down the western shore of Lake Michigan, they encountered a storm at night and did not get ashore until the morning of September 20. If La Salle's group had departed from Washington, Detroit, Rock, or Plum Island such a situation would have been impossible. It is only about 4 miles from Washington or Detroit Island to Door Peninsula, where the western shore of Lake Michigan begins. It is even less from there to Plum Island. However, the canoe route from Summer Island bay to this part of Lake Michigan shore is about 30 miles, and a voyage by canoe from Summer Island to the mainland in Door County, Wisconsin, would very well fit Hennepin's description of events on the night of September 19, 1679. Consequently, considering all of the lines of evidence known to me, I would choose Summer Island as the Island of the Potawatomis which was visited by La Salle and Hennepin in the *Griffin* in early September of 1679.

THE FATE OF THE GRIFFIN

The *Griffin*, loaded with furs for the European markets, set sail from the Island of the Potawatomis on September 18, 1679, downward bound for the east end of Lake Erie. En route she disappeared and was never seen again. Hennepin said the *Griffin* was lost in a storm on northern Lake Michigan. Writing at a later time, Bacqueville de la Potherie (Blair, 1911, I, 353) stated that the *Griffin*, driven by a storm "into a small bay, five or six leagues from the anchorage which it had left," was boarded by a party of Ottawa Indians who killed the crew and burned the ship. This statement, made so long after the fact, might have been based on knowledge of a letter written by La Salle to La Barre on June 4,

1683 (see Parkman, 1894, p. 301). In the letter La Salle expresses the belief that the *Griffin* was destroyed by the pilot and some of the crew, who then attempted to join Du Lhut, but were captured by Indians. If Bacqueville de la Potherie's account is correct, the *Griffin* met its end in northern Lake Michigan in one of the bays south of Point aux Barques, probably in Delta County, Michigan. Just which of these bays it might have been depends in part on the exact identification of the Island of the Potawatomis from which the *Griffin* sailed. Since I favor the identification of Summer Island as the Island of the Potawatomis, I would expect the Portage Bay area to be the place where the *Griffin* disappeared, if I accepted the account of Bacqueville de la Potherie. However, I accept Father Hennepin's account of the matter and will therefore reach a somewhat different conclusion.

Hennepin was in the region for several years after the disappearance of the *Griffin* and should have had a chance to pick up any information, rumors, or gossip about the vessel in the French establishments near Green Bay or at Michilimackinac. In March of 1680, according to Parkman (1894, p. 179), the two men La Salle had sent in search of the missing vessel reported to him that they had made a circuit of Lake Michigan and "had neither seen her nor heard tidings of her." Hennepin spent the winter of 1680–81 among the Indians and Frenchmen at Michilimackinac, where he might have acquired some of the information he relates, but of many of the events of 1679 he was an eye witness. According to Hennepin (1698, Chap. 22, pp. 89–90):

M. la Salle, without asking anybody's Advice, resolv'd to send back his Ship to Niagara, laden with Furrs [sic] and Skins to discharge his Debts; our Pilot and five Men with him were therefore sent back, and order'd to return with all imaginable speed, to join us toward the Southern Parts of the Lake, where we should stay for them among the Illinois. They sailed the 18th of September with a Westerly Wind, and fir'd a Gun [cannon] to take their leave. Tho' the Wind was favorable [blowing from a direction that would enable them to steer a direct course without tacking], it was never known what Course they steer'd, nor how they perished; for after all the Enquiries we have been able to make, we could never learn any thing else but the following Particulars.

The Ship came to an Anchor to the North of the Lake of the Illinois [Lake Michigan], where he [sic] was seen by some Savages, who told us that they advised our Men to sail along the Coast, and not towards the middle of the Lake, because of the Sands [shoals, bars, islands] that make the Navigation dangerous when there is any high Wind. Our Pilot, as I said before, was dissatisfy'd and would steer as he pleas'd, without hearkning to the Advice of the Savages, who, generally speaking, have more Sense than the Europeans think at first; but the Ship was hardly a League from the Coast, when it was toss'd up by a violent Storm in such a manner, that our Men were never heard of since; and it is suppos'd that the Ship struck upon a Sand was there bury'd.

When the *Griffin* left the Island of the Potawatomis on September 18, 1679, the wind was westerly; that is to say it was blowing from a direction somewhere between northwest and southwest, but not directly from the west. The wind was also favorable, which is to say it was a following or near following wind in relation to the course the *Griffin* had to sail, and since the *Griffin*'s course should have been northeasterly the favorable westerly wind on September 18, 1679, must have been blowing from a point between west and southwest or from the southwest.

Additional information about the wind and weather for September 19–25, 1679, in northern Lake Michigan, can be gleaned from Father Hennepin's account of the beginning of his canoe journey from the Island of the Potawatomis southward down the Wisconsin shore of Lake Michigan. On September 19 the weather was mild, but the wind increased during the night and it was stormy for the next four days (Hennepin, 1698, Chap. 22, pp. 91–92) — from September 20 through September 24. The wind and waves were so great that Hennepin and La Salle's party had to remain on shore during this period. Their position in relation to the Lake Michigan shore of Wisconsin's Door Peninsula would have protected them from winds blowing from due north, northwest, west, and southwest; therefore, the winds that kept La Salle's group storm-bound on the shore must have come from the south, southeast, east, or northeast. Moreover, the weather conditions that prevailed for four days near the southern entrance into Green Bay would have been general over the whole northern Lake Michigan area. And whether the wind was from the south, southeast, east, or northeast, the *Griffin* was in potential trouble, for there were no harbors or protected anchorages along the northern shore of Lake Michigan. Sooner or later she would be helpless either on a lee shore or on rocks and shoals offshore.

On the basis of my own experience in uncharted waters I would expect that after the *Griffin* departed from the Island of the Potawatomis on September 18, 1679, the pilot would have steered a northeasterly course following the shore. The favorable westerly wind probably died with the setting of the sun, which would have been fairly early at this time of year, but even if the wind had continued during the night it would have been very dangerous to continue the voyage blindly through the uncharted waters of northern Lake Michigan. I would believe Hennepin's statement that the *Griffin* anchored in the northern end of Lake Michigan. This anchorage most likely would have been in the vicinity of Manistique, Michigan, or between Manistique and Seul Choix Point. On September 19, according to Hennepin, the weather was calm and the *Griffin* may have remained at anchor or may have been able to move a short distance, but was still west of Seul Choix Point. In such a position the vessel was safe in a northeasterly gale but hopelessly lost in a southerly storm. If the *Griffin* had ventured out past the protection of Seul Choix Point and had been caught in a northeasterly gale she would have been blown southwestward and wrecked in the vicinity of Point Aux Barques.

If by the night of September 19, 1679, the *Griffin* had been coasting as far east as Epoufette, Michigan, she would have been wrecked on a lee shore with a storm from the south or wrecked at sea or in the Beaver Islands in a storm from the north or northeast. If we ignore Hennepin's statement about the *Griffin* reaching an anchorage in northern Lake Michigan, we would then assume that when the vessel departed from the Island of the Potawatomis she headed directly to sea in an easterly direction. The *Griffin*, a slow sailor to judge from her performance on Lake Erie and Lake Huron, might have reached the Beaver Islands by nightfall but would have become hopelessly enmeshed in shoals and islands if she tried to proceed in the dark. The lack of wind on September 19 and the complicated nature of the passage through or around the Beaver Islands would suggest that had the *Griffin* taken the easterly course from the Island of the Potawatomis she would have been somewhere in the vicinity of the Beaver Islands at the beginning of the storm in northern Lake Michigan the night of September 19, 1679. In such a position the *Griffin* would probably have been wrecked somewhere among the Beaver Islands. If the storm was from the south and the *Griffin* was north of the Beavers she might have been blown northward and wrecked somewhere between Seul Choix Point and Epoufette, perhaps at Mille Coquins. With the *Griffin* in the same position a storm from any other direction would have wrecked her among the Beaver Islands.

Whatever happened to the *Griffin* it seems almost certain that she never got as far east as St. Ignace after leaving the Island of the Potawatomis. And, regardless of what else might have taken place, it seems unreasonable to believe that the *Griffin* could have survived the storm on northern Lake Michigan that lasted from the night of September 19 through September 24, 1679. Just how terrible a storm can be on northern Lake Michigan is exemplified by the loss of the freighter, *Carl D. Bradley*, in November of 1958. Many, many times larger than the *Griffin*, the *Bradley* was 640 feet long and capable of carrying 18,000 tons of cargo. Nonetheless, she was no match for the 20 to 30 foot waves pushed by southwest winds of 65 miles an hour velocity. She broke in half and sank in 365 feet of water off the western edge of the Beaver Island archipelago. The force of wind and waves was so great that it took the 250-foot German freighter, *Christian Sartori*, two hours to cover the four miles between their position and the place where the *Bradley* sank (Ratigan, 1960, pp. 16–35). To imagine the plight of the *Griffin* in September of 1679 one need only look at a detailed maritime chart of northern Lake Michigan and think of the magnitude of the autumnal storm that sank the *Bradley* in 1958.

If I were to search for possible remains of the *Griffin*, I would first look beneath the coastal waters of Delta and Schoolcraft counties in Michigan between Point Detour and Seul Choix Point, particularly around Point Aux Barques and the site of the old settlement at Seul Choix. I would next check the coastal waters eastward as far as Epoufette in Mackinac County, Michigan, and, finally, I would search all the shoals in the Beaver Island archipelago.

That the *Griffin* disappeared without trace is no surprise if she was destroyed in the storm of September 19–24, 1679. Nor is it surprising that ships like the *Griffin* did not replace canoes as cargo carriers on the upper Great Lakes during the major part of the fur trade era. The only advantages that a boat like the *Griffin* had over a large freight canoe or a brigade of such canoes

Fig. 10. — Canoe freighter of about 1820 on northern Lake Huron. Courtesy of Chicago Natural History Museum.

was that the boat was a floating fortress and required fewer men for the amount of freight handled. These advantages, however, were far outweighed by the lack of harbors, the numerous hazards to navigation, and the lack of marine charts. Whereas a boat like the *Griffin* was always at the mercy of a storm, a freight canoe could put ashore almost anywhere. The large Montreal canoes (Fig. 10) that became the real freighters of the fur trade era were never replaced by sailing ships. Such a canoe 35 to 40 feet long could carry 5 tons of crew and freight and, with fourteen men, could make 4 to 6 miles an hour in calm weather and 8 to 10 miles per hour with a favorable wind and sail plus paddles (see Nute, 1931, pp. 23–28). Thus an Indian invention, the birchbark canoe, became, with some French modification, the ideal commercial vessel during the era of the fur trade on the upper Great Lakes.

REFERENCES

Blair, 1911; Glasgow, 1964; Griffin, 1943; Hennepin, 1698; Morison, 1925; Nute, 1931; Parkman, 1894; Ratigan, 1960; Tucker, 1942.

CHAPTER 5

DATING THE PAST WITH JEW'S-HARPS,
JESUIT RINGS, AND OTHER TRADE OBJECTS

Time is most important to the archaeologist, because whatever else he does, he must discover the temporal relationships of the cultures he describes and order them in proper sequence from earliest to latest. To do all this the archaeologist may make use of stratigraphic position or radiocarbon dating or some other means of establishing temporal order. Neither stratigraphic position nor radiocarbon measurement seems to work well within the framework of the archaeology of the historic period. The probable error in the radiocarbon dating is too great for the brief sequences and general recency of the historic period. The scattered sites and shallow deposits of occupational debris characteristic of the historic period in the western Great Lakes region do not easily lend themselves to stratigraphic analysis. It thus seems obvious that some other means of dating is needed here. The ideal dating system would be simple historical documentation — a dated map of great accuracy or a document testifying that in a given year Mr. X, a man of unimpeachable veracity, visited a specific Indian village at a specific spot that can easily be located at the present time. Unfortunately this ideal situation does not exist in the western Great Lakes region. With a few possible exceptions in Ontario (Huronia) the Indian sites of the historic period in this region are lacking adequate historical documentation. It therefore becomes necessary to use a special way of dating historic period sites, namely the presence or absence of certain kinds of trade goods.

Trade objects consisted of material things used by white men in the fur trade with the Indians. Some of these were made either in Europe or in Colonial America especially for trade, while others were regular European items for which there was a demand on the part of the Indians. For instance, in the summer of 1679 when the *Griffin* sailed into northern Lake Michigan there was on board a considerable quantity of European goods intended for trade with the Indians. The writings of Father Louis Hennepin (1698, I, *passim*) provide a record of the goods that were traded, which I list in the following paragraphs.

Trade goods made of iron were axes, hatchets, knives, shoemaker's awls or bodkins, needles, fishhooks, fire forks, and pothooks. There were also "iron tools to cultivate" (hoes), shovels, and even pickaxes. Most shovels and pickaxes, however, probably were not intended for use as items of exchange in the fur trade at this particular time.

There were flintlock muskets, known to Father Hennepin as fusils, bullets, gunpowder, bottles for gunpowder (when they were emptied of wine or brandy), and undoubtedly large quantities of gunflints, although these were not mentioned specifically. Some idea of the value of a flintlock gun is provided by Hennepin's statement that his companion traded one fusil for a birchbark canoe.

Large quantities of brandy and Martinico tobacco were carried for purposes of trade. A roll of tobacco 7 yards long is described in one place, and in another is mentioned a roll weighing 50 pounds. There is, however, no mention of European tobacco pipes.

Kettles were common items of trade. They were probably made of brass, though Father Hennepin neglected to mention the material in his writings. For his own use he had an iron pot three feet around with the figure of a lion on it, an item which some upper Mississippi Valley Indians refused to accept in trade. Other trade goods consisted of looking glasses and "little toys," meaning nonutilitarian or inexpensive items such as brass rings, jew's-harps, combs, and the like.

European textile goods carried for trade with Indians included cloaks, shirts, "pieces of fine cloth," and handkerchiefs of "Armenian" cloth. European items not directly connected with the fur trade, but nonetheless present in the region, according to Father Hennepin, were a pewter flagon for wine, ornaments of the chapel, a steel box for documents and other things, religious medals, pencil and paper, ice skates, drugs (powder of orvietan and Mithridate), and herbs (purslain, pulse, and sweet marjoram).

Glass beads were a very important medium of exchange in the fur trade. Father Hennepin mentions collars of white and blue beads, bracelets of little black and white beads, colored glass beads shaped like pearls or little rings, and little glass beads.

A list of the trade goods taken into the Illinois country by a fur trader in 1688 (see Bauxar, 1959, p. 47) contains the following: 25 ells linen, of three grades (an ell equals a yard plus 9 inches); 15 ells scarlet cloth; 19.5 ells serge for capes; 18.5 ells red serge for capes; 13 capes, of two grades; 8 livres sewing thread (a livre as a unit of weight equals 1 pound); 24 pair stockings, of two grades; 26 dozen butcher knives, of two sizes; 6 dozen canoe knives; 2 dozen clasp knives; 36 dozen hatchets, of two sizes; 2 large axes; 8 muskets, of two qualities; 100 livres gunpowder; 200 livres lead; 71 livres of lead balls; 8 gun pliers; 200 musket flints; 1 livre gun worms; 100 arrowheads of iron; 30 augers; 24 steels for striking fire; 65 livres copper (brass) kettles; 5 livres glass beads; 200 quills; 4 dozen paints; 2.25 livres azure blue; 12 mirrors; 8.5 livres thread for nets; 64 livres tobacco; 25 livres brandy; and 2 minots (68.66 quarts) peas.

A number of trade objects and their values were included in a list of the expenses incurred by the French in their war with the Fox Indians in 1715–16 (see Brown, 1918, pp. 70–89 *passim*). The objects mentioned include small axes at 3 livres each (a livre as a monetary unit was the equivalent of a franc or a shilling of later times); medium-sized axes at 9 livres each; large axes at 13 livres 10 sols; fire steels at 108 livres a gross; 2 flintlock guns at 40 livres each; 12 flintlock guns at 30 livres each; 2,820 gunflints at 3 livres 15 sols per 100; gun worms at 20 livres a gross; iron hoes at 10 livres 10 sols each; knives at 54 livres a gross; Flemish knives at 127 livres 10 sols a gross; horn-handled clasp knives at 6 livres a dozen; lance blades at 25 livres 4 sols a gross; more than 22,000 (glass) porcelain beads at 10 livres per thousand; and 2 pounds of rassade (glass) beads at 4 livres 10 sols.

Another list of trade goods — one used by the Hudson's Bay Company in 1748 (see Woodward, 1948, p. 5) — was as follows: large milk beads; beads of colors; beads of all sorts; brass kettles of all sizes; black lead; powder; shot; brown sugar; Brazil tobacco; leaf tobacco; roll tobacco; thread; powdered vermilion; English brandy; white or red waters (fortified wines); red, white, or blue broadcloth; fine blue broadcloth; red or blue bays (baize); blankets; red, white, or blue duffels; flannel; gartering; broad Orris lace; worsted binding; awl blades; coat buttons; waistcoat buttons; cargo breeches; burning glasses; bayonets; ivory combs; egg boxes; barrel boxes; red feathers; fishhooks; fire steels (strike-a-lights); large flat files; French gunflints; flintlock guns of 3, 3.5, or 4 foot length; pistols; gun worms; yarn gloves; goggles; handkerchiefs; laced hats; hatchets; hawk bells; ice chisels; knives; looking glasses; crooked knives; needles; net lines; powder horns; plain rings; plain, seal, or stone-set rings; runlets (small barrels) of 2 quart, 3 quart, 1 gallon, 2 gallon, and 3 gallon capacities; sword blades; scrapers; scissors; spoons; shirts; shoes; stockings; worsted sashes; brass thimbles; tobacco boxes; tobacco tongs; red leather trunks; twine; and cottons.

A very much later list, 1804–1806, of annuity goods and purchases, taken from the daybooks of the factory at Fort Wayne, Indiana (see Baerreis, 1961, pp. 62–67), contains a number of items received by Potawatomi or Miami Indians. These items consist of horse gear, such as saddles, bridles, cruppers, surcingles, saddlebags, bells and bell straps, curb bridle bits, and horse collars; flintlock rifles; gunflints; gunpowder; lead; gunlocks; powder horns; shot pouches; a steel trap; canteens; knives; pocket knives; scalping knives; brass kettles; tin kettles; tin cups; jacks (metal pitchers); wire; tin pans; pewter teapot; trunk; padlocks; large hinges; foot adzes; hoes; augers; gimlets; nails; frying pan; spoon; axes; corn mill; handsaw; silver brooches; silver headbands; silver wristbands; silver ear wheels; vermilion paint; looking glasses; comb; pomatum (sticks); wampum (carried in stock, but not purchased); feathers (the same); hats; cloth leggings; shirts; belts; handkerchiefs; blankets; moccasins; breechcloth; yard goods; ferret (band of flowered silk); ribbons; thread; needles; silk and cotton stockings; dressed skins; morning gown; tobacco; pipes; snuffbox; jew's-harps; brimstone; soap; salt; potatoes; corn; tea; pepper; and allspice.

Although these lists give us some knowledge of the classes of objects traded and their change through time, neither Father Hennepin nor any other European of the period described trade goods in detail sufficient to meet the standards desired by archaeologists. And although it is useful and necessary to consult such lists, much more detailed information has been obtained from archaeological sources. For instance, trade objects found with Huron burials in Huronia must represent a period earlier than 1650 because by that date the Hurons had abandoned the area. Similarly trade goods found at Fort Michilimackinac in northern Michigan and in the environs of Fort St. Joseph in southern Michigan can be attributed to the first three quarters of the eighteenth century. Objects from dated occupancies outside of the region can be used to help establish a chronology based on trade goods. For example, French-dominated sites in the lower Mississippi Valley historically dated between 1680 and 1750 have yielded trade objects that were the same as those found at Forts Michilimackinac and St. Joseph dating from the French occupancy. Thus by studying assemblages of trade objects from archaeological sites of known date I have been able to construct a regional chronology of trade goods. By the presence of diagnostic assemblages of trade goods it is possible to estimate the dates of undocumented Indian sites of the historic period.

As noted in Chapter 1, I have found it convenient at the present time to divide the entire historic period into three segments: the Early Historic period (1610 to 1670), the Middle Historic period (1670 to 1760), and the Late Historic period (1760 to 1820). Preferably there should be more and shorter divisions, but this scheme is the best I can produce at the moment. During the Early Historic period the French were the dominant European group in the western Great Lakes. In the Middle Historic period the French dominated not only the western Great Lakes but the entire Mississippi Valley. During the Late Historic period the western Great

Lakes region was under British domination, and at the beginning of this latest period there was a relatively radical shift from French to British sponsored trade objects.

The kinds of trade objects most likely to be found in undocumented village and burial sites of the Indians of the historic period are glass beads, silver ornaments, iron knives, brass pots and kettles, white kaolin pipes, iron axes, glass bottles, gunflints, flintlock guns, brass rings, lead baling or fabric seals, iron hoes, religious medals, jew's-harps, iron awls, fishhooks, needles, thimbles, scissors, mirrors, and Chinese and European porcelain and china. Because of the amount of accumulated information about them and their importance in dating historic period sites, the glass beads and silver ornaments have been described in Chapters 6 and 7. Other trade objects are discussed in this chapter.

Iron clasp-knife blades 4 or 5 inches long, with French names stamped on them, are representative of the Early and Middle Historic periods (see Quimby, 1939, p. 27, and Maxwell and Binford, 1961, pp. 105–6). Despite considerable variation, each of these knives can be classed in one of two major types — those with sharply pointed blades or those with blades shaped somewhat like the bill of a hawk (Fig. 11). All have a horizontal transverse flange at the top of the butt of the blade and a hole through the blade at the basal end. All of these blades originally had impressed upon them the names of their makers — for example, JEAN B. TIVET, IVET. CHAPELON, JEAN PERRIOT, ANTOINE. PER, I. ROVET, PIERRE THOMAS LE JUNE, A. POLIVET, CLAUDI, PIERRE. PERE N. LE FIL, JEAN ARCONE, ANTOINE, JEAN BARME, HUGUE PALLE (with a flower), CLAUDE PERRIN, TERNE. PER ET FIL, A. FELI, AUDE. EVRANDE, I. C. DORON, A. PEREN LE JEUNE, AERAOL. LAYN, BARTELEMY PERRIN, and JEAN ERIOL — but in most cases pitting from rust has obliterated the manufacturer's name.

Although various forms of iron butcher knives were present in the Early and Middle Historic periods they are not particularly useful in dating these temporal segments because they have not been carefully studied. Moreover, the French clasp-knife blade characteristic of these two periods is at present a better indicator of these early times. Butcher knives of the Middle Historic period can be recognized because they have French names stamped on the blade. In other respects they seem to be the same as or similar to butcher knives found in dated sites of the Late Historic period. In the Late Historic period the French clasp knife is lacking and the rarely found British type of clasp-knife blade is recognizable because it has a split hinge at the basal end. However, in this late period several or more butcher knives may be present in a given Indian site, but never in association with French clasp knives. Thus, in terms of dating, one can expect that a find of butcher knives and French clasp knives in combination are diagnostic of the Early and Middle Historic periods and butcher knives alone are generally indicative of the Late Historic period.

Iron axes and hatchets of various weights and sizes are found in sites from all three of the divisions of the historic period, and

Fig. 11. — Iron knife blades and fragments of eared kettles of brass typical of the Middle Historic period, 1670–1760. After Wittry (1963).

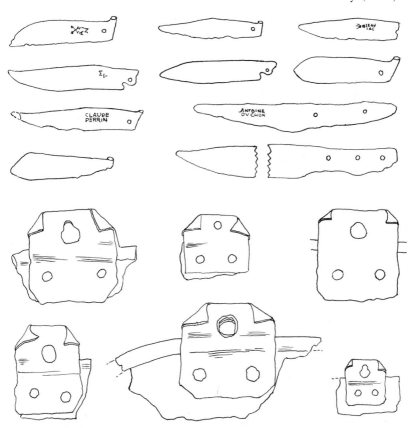

Fig. 12. — Some French trade goods of the Middle Historic period, 1670–1760, from sites in the lower Mississippi Valley. Courtesy of the Chicago Natural History Museum. *Top row*: iron axes and iron hoes. *Middle row*: brass hawk bells, a tinkling cone of kettle brass, a brass bracelet, and more hawk bells of brass. *Bottom row*: fragments of china, a glass bottle neck, round-heel gunflints, an oval strike-a-light, a jew's-harp, and a gun barrel sawed open to show lead ball in firing position.

I am unable to recognize differences in style that should exist. All axes appear to have been forged of strap iron over a wedge-shaped center piece (Fig. 12). The sides of the blades frequently have stamped impressions consisting of crosses or conventionalized blossom shapes in a round cartouche. The steel tomahawk-pipes, consisting of a hatchet blade and pipe bowl combined, are a European invention and are confined to the Late Historic period. Some of these were quite elaborate, with engraved, inlaid, or pierced blades and engraved pipe bowls.

Iron hoes (Fig. 12) of various sizes seem to be most characteristic of the Middle Historic period. These had flat blades with a loop socket apparently made of an iron strap. Some of the larger-sized hoes could have been used as mattocks. Iron pots with ornamental designs or with three legs (Fig. 13) are uncommon but

Fig. 13. — Brass kettles, an iron kettle with three legs, and an earthenware jug representative of the Middle Historic period, 1670–1760. Courtesy of Chicago Natural History Museum.

nonetheless representative of the Middle Historic period. In the Late Historic period, a large iron kettle with rounded bottom was used for boiling maple sap (see Fig. 33) and is characteristic of that period.

C-shaped bracelets made of various gauges of brass wire (see Fig. 12) are diagnostic of the Early and Middle Historic periods, in contrast to the Late Historic period when bracelets were made of sheet silver.

Brass pots and kettles of different sizes (Fig. 13) are representative of all three divisions of the historic period. A canister type with a cover seems to have been present only in the Late Historic period sites. Those brass kettles with two square or rectangular lugs were common in the Middle Historic period, but are not necessarily diagnostic. The lugs were made of two or more thicknesses of sheet brass and were attached to the kettle bowls with two large rivets, usually of lead. The two upper corners of the lugs were bent over from right (or nearly so) triangles and hammered flat (Fig. 11). This procedure reinforced the top part of the lug and eliminated sharp corners. An iron bail (handle) was inserted through a hole in each lug. Some large lugs, detached from kettles and showing wear and polish on the bottom edge, may have been used as hoes. Such have been found in Indian sites of the Middle Historic period. But battered lugs and fragments of brass from kettles are frequently present in sites dating from any one of the three divisions of the historic period.

Objects made of sheet brass obtained from broken kettles consisted of tubular beads, hair pipes, conical tinklers (Figs. 12 and 14), and arrowheads of two forms. The tubular beads were made of small rolled-up squares of sheet brass. The hair pipes were similar to the beads but much larger. The conical tinklers were made of rolled up trapezoidal sections of sheet brass that were fastened to buckskin fringes to give a tinkling sound with motion. The arrowheads were either conical or flat triangular in shape. These artifacts are not trade goods, yet they were fashioned from a foreign material obtained by trade with white men, so I have included them here. They are typical of the entire historic period, but most abundant in sites of the Middle Historic period. The brass arrowheads are rare or lacking in the Late Historic period of the western Great Lakes region.

Fig. 14. — Brass tinkling cones attached to a leather bag ornamented with embroidery of dyed porcupine quills. This bag, now in Chicago Natural History Museum, was acquired by Jeffrey Amherst between 1758 and 1763.

Glass bottles of several kinds are often found in Indian village and burial sites of the historic period. Except for those in Late Historic period sites the bottles are usually in fragments, but the upper portions alone of long-necked bottles are excellent indicators of period. Such bottles have an appliqué ring of glass around the neck and beneath the lip (Fig. 12). In the Early and Middle Historic periods this ring is always beneath the lip; the lower it is, the earlier the bottle. By the beginning of the Late Historic period this ring is adjacent to the lip, or consists of a molded flat ring or double ring adjoining the lip. Many of these long-necked bottles are wine bottles with body styles that change significantly at rather short intervals within the historic period (see Hudson, 1962, pp. 6–9), but since neck fragments are more plentiful than whole or restorable bottles in most Indian sites, it is easier to use the attribute of ring position for dating purposes, especially when dealing with the relatively long temporal divisions that I have proposed.

Rectangular bottles called case bottles or gin bottles, with short necks and without appliqué rings, are characteristic of the Middle Historic period. They are easily recognized, even by fragments, because of their square bottoms and square-cornered bodies. Bottles of this type are made of various shades of light green glass.

Glass bottles of the Late Historic period are often of molded glass as well as of blown glass. The flat ring or double ring at the lip is the best criterion for identification of the long-necked bottles of this period, but there are also ornate molded flasks and polychrome enameled bottles, such as those made by Heinrich Stiegal of Pennsylvania in the late eighteenth century, that are diagnostic of the Late Historic period. Small patent medicine bottles are also diagnostic of this period. These are round or square in cross section, with short necks and flaring lips, or they may be fiddle-shaped. Some of them have raised letters indicating their contents, such as ESSENCE OF PEPPERMINT BY THE KINGS PATENT or BY THE KINGS ROYAL PATENT GRANTED TO ROBT. TURLINGTON FOR HIS INVENTED BALSOM OF LIFE. The spelling is not always consistent. Of two bottles from the same grave, one spelled *peppermint* with three *p*'s, the other with two *p*'s.

Porcelain and chinaware (Fig. 12) are more characteristic of the ruins of forts and trading establishments (see Maxwell and

Binford, 1961, pp. 92–95) than of Indian village and burial sites, except in the Late Historic period. Those sites in use between 1760 and 1820 produce many varieties of English pottery of Stafford-shire or similar style with transfer printed designs. Early and Middle Historic period sites in the western Great Lakes region seem to lack the European pottery and Chinese blue and white porcelain that have been found in the ruins of forts and trading posts. However, in other contexts outside of the western Great Lakes region European ceramics are of great importance in the specific datings of various kinds of Indian and Colonial sites (see South, 1962; Fairbanks, 1962; and Powell, 1962). Glazed jugs of earthenware (Fig. 13) seem to have been most popular in the Middle Historic period.

Flintlock guns are characteristic of the Middle and Late Historic periods (see Hamilton, 1960). Although guns and parts of guns (Fig. 12) have a potential for use in dating, gunflints are far bet-ter at the present time because they are more sensitive indicators of chronology. Millions of gunflints must have been imported into America, and they are often found in the village sites, camp sites, and graves of the Indians. Gunflints were used to ignite the black powder charge in the guns, and because they became worn or were lost or used for other purposes gunflints were always in demand and always present in relatively large quantities. Gunflints of spall type with rounded heel (Fig. 12) are diagnostic of the Middle Historic period and perhaps the last part of the Early Historic period. These are almost always made of blond or brown flint and were imported from France (see Hamilton, 1960; and Smith, 1961). In the last part of the Middle Historic period and the early part of the Late Historic period there are both prismlike (blade) gunflints with round heels made of blond flint and rec-tangular prismlike (blade) gunflints with square heels made of black or gray flint, although the older spall form may also be present. But the gunflint truly diagnostic of the Late Historic peri-od, regardless of what other gunflints are present in an assemblage, is this English-made dark-colored prismatic form with the square heel or back.

Baling seals made of lead are diagnostic of the Middle Historic period. These have also been called fabric seals, and were attached to the brass wires that held bundles of trade blankets (see Maxwell and Binford, 1961, p. 89, and Quimby, 1939, p. 27). Many of the seals have dates stamped on them. Although lead baling seals are most often found at sites of forts and trading establishments, I have included them here because they have been found occasionally in Indian sites and they are excellent indicators of time.

There are a number of miscellaneous trade objects that are indicative of the historic period in general and for which I cannot yet detect any specific changes from one temporal division to another within the historic period. These trade objects include steel strike-a-lights (Fig. 12), needles, several kinds of iron awls, eyeless fishhooks of iron, powdered vermilion for paint, jew's-harps with frames of iron or brass (Fig. 12), mirrors, magnifying or burning glasses, scissors, iron fish spears, brass thimbles, Morris or hawk bells of brass (Fig. 12) and brass tinkling cones (Fig. 14), which were attached to clothing, wristbands and anklets, and bags. Some of the brass thimbles seem to have also been used as tinklers attached to fringes of clothing.

Religious medals of various sorts are characteristic of the Early and Middle Historic periods in the upper Great Lakes region (see Kidd, 1949, Fig. 23, and Quimby, 1939, p. 27). Usually these medals are made of bronze. They are oval or octagonal in outline and on obverse and reverse bear depictions of saints, religious inscriptions in Latin or French, and various symbols. Examples of inscriptions are "St. Ignace," "St. Anna," "Infant and Holy Mother," "St. Rosa," "St. Ignatius," "St. Matthia," "St. Magdale," "St. Francis," "St. Benedict," "Soc Iesu," "Beatus. Ignias. Loiola. Auctor. et Funda. Societa Iesu," and "Par votre mort et votre sépulture déliverez nous Jésus." In all likelihood these medals or medallions were presented to Indian converts by missionaries, many of whom were Jesuits. Such medallions seem to be completely lacking in the Indian sites of the Late Historic period.

Jesuit rings, so called (Fig. 15), are excellent chronological indicators of the Middle Historic period. These are brass rings with heart-shaped, oval, octagonal, round, and other forms of bezels upon which are crudely engraved religious symbols (see Quimby, 1939, p. 26). Some characteristic symbols engraved on these rings are the following: IHS and a cross, a heart and crown, a tonsured priest with cross, N, IN, NI, XX, IXXI, FI, IF, I, IB, CB, slashed hearts, bleeding hearts, VI, AI, crescents, and a number of others. A small thin ring of brass set with bits of clear or colored glass is also a diagnostic trait of the Middle Historic period.

Various kinds of pendants which at first glance seem to be of native manufacture but which probably were made by white men for the fur trade with Indians are characteristic of the Middle Historic period. These include V-shaped objects and beaver effigies of catlinite, perforated for suspension, and shell runtees which are disks with two parallel holes made with a fine drill through the long section of the disk. The face of the runtee has an engraved design consisting of dot and circle and other motifs made with a steel compass.

Fragments of kaolin pipes are frequently found in historic sites, particularly those of the Middle and Late Historic periods. In their day these white clay pipes were abundant and expendable; and when broken, the fragments endured in good shape down to the present time. Pipe fragments have been found by the hundreds at forts, trading establishments, and the beginning of well-traveled portages. To a much lesser degree the fragments of these white clay pipes are present in the village, camp, and burial sites of the Indians of the upper Great Lakes region. The pipes repre-

Fig. 15 — Changes in fastenings of metal buttons and symbols engraved on Jesuit finger rings of brass. Rings are of styles found at the Bell site, Fort St. Joseph, and Fort Michilimackinac. Courtesy of Chicago Natural History Museum.

sented by these fragments may be dated in three different ways. One way is to utilize the names, initials, marks, or other insignia that were stamped on the pipes by their makers at the time of manufacture. In a number of cases the pipe-maker can be identified; and by determining through historical research the years during which he worked, the approximate date of the manufacture of the pipe can be ascertained. For instance, the mark "WB" on a pipe could indicate that the pipe was made in England by William Bachelor between 1600 and 1640. A pipe stamped with the initials "LE" could have been made by Luellin Evans of Bristol between the years 1661 and about 1691. Similarly pipe-makers in France, Holland, Scotland, and America had signs and marks that can aid in identifying the maker and dating the pipe.

Another way to date clay pipes is by their change in form over the years. In the early seventeenth century the pipe bowls were bulbous, later in the same century they were barrel-shaped, and about 1690 to 1750 the bowls became elongated and thinner with gently curving to almost straight side-walls. In this span of time the angle between bowl and stem gradually became less and less obtuse (see Omwake, 1958). But there is a third and most simple way of dating pipes, based on the diameter of the hole or bore in the stems (see Harrington, 1954; Omwake, 1958; and Binford, 1962). This third method of dating pipes is based on the fact that the stem holes or bores were largest in the earliest pipes and smallest in the latest with a gradual decrease in size between the two extremes. The stem hole or bore diameters of the Early Historic period range from $\frac{9}{64}$ to $\frac{7}{64}$ inch. In the first half of the period more than 50 per cent of the stem holes were $\frac{8}{64}$ inch in diameter, and in the second half more than 50 per cent of the stem holes were $\frac{7}{64}$ inch in diameter. In the Middle Historic period more than 70 per cent of the stem hole diameters were either $\frac{6}{64}$ or $\frac{5}{64}$ inch. And in the Late Historic period the presence of large quantities of stems with bore diameters of $\frac{4}{64}$ inch are diagnostic regardless of what other stem hole diameters may be included in the assemblage of pipe fragments from a given site.

Plain metal buttons, when found in an Indian site, are good chronological indicators (see Olsen, 1963). Those typical of the Middle Historic period were of cast brass, bronze, pewter, or white metal with a wedge-shaped cast shank in which there was a drilled hole (Fig. 15). Several styles of plain metal buttons were characteristic of the Late Historic period. One type was of cast white metal with a heavy eye, cast at the same time as the button (Fig. 15). Another type cast of white metal or brass had a brass-wire eye set into a boss (Fig. 15). A burred edge on the boss where the ring eye connected and concentric tool marks on the back of the button were additional characteristics of this style. Still another type consisted of a button cast of white metal with an iron wire shank or eye let into a boss on the back of the button which was marked by a mold seam and plug (Fig. 15).

In the dating of an Indian village, camp, or burial site one must consider the entire assemblage of trade objects, remembering, of course, that older types of objects are often kept as heirlooms or for other reasons, and that the date of a given assemblage is the date of the youngest trade object present. Excavation of an Indian site might produce a few chevron beads, religious medals, pipe stems with whole diameters of $\frac{9}{64}$ inch, iron arrowheads, brass kettles, and necks of glass bottles with appliqué rings low on the neck, accompanied by aboriginal pottery, flint arrowheads, stone axes, and shell beads. Such an assemblage would be recognized immediately as a phenomenon of the Early Historic period, by means of the dating system utilizing the association of trade objects.

An Indian site dated in the Middle Historic period might contain numerous glass beads of the many styles diagnostic of the period, spall type gunflints with rounded heels, iron clasp knives with French names on them, jew's-harps, Jesuit finger rings, wine bottles, and many other trade objects, in association with native pottery, pipes, some stone tools, and a few flint arrowheads.

Another Indian site might, on excavation, show evidence of numerous silver ornaments, parts of flintlock guns, bottle necks with a flat ring at the lip, jew's-harps, dark-colored gunflints of prism type with squared heel, patent medicine bottles, Stafford-shire style pottery, kaolin pipe stems with bores of $\frac{4}{64}$ inch in diameter, and many other trade objects, accompanied by artifacts of native manufacture such as wooden bowls and ladles, bone harpoon heads, bone matting needles, and sheets of birchbark. From the nature of the associated trade objects one would place this site in the Late Historic period that began in 1760.

This method — described here in simplified form — of determining unknown dates by associated trade objects of known date is the means used in later chapters to place undocumented Indian sites in their proper divisions of the historic period.

REFERENCES

Baerreis, 1961; Bauxar, 1959; Binford, 1962; Brown, 1918; Fairbanks, 1962; Hamilton, 1960; Harrington, 1954; Hennepin, 1698; Hudson, 1962; Kidd, 1949; Maxwell and Binford, 1961; Olsen, 1963; Omwake, 1958; Powell, 1962; Quimby, 1938, 1939, 1942; Smith, 1961; South, 1962; Woodward, 1948.

CHAPTER 6

CHRONOLOGY FROM GLASS BEADS

Beads of various sorts have been in use among the Indians of North America for thousands of years. The European discoverers and conquerors of America were quick to recognize the Indians' desire for beads and were equally quick to exploit this desire in the differing contact situations that occurred in the historic period. European beads made of glass were used as presents to obtain the good will of Indians or were used in trade for the purchase of land, furs, food, and other things considered valuable by the white men.

The first recorded use of trade beads was that of Christopher Columbus on October 12 and 15, 1492. In his log it is stated that

In order to win the friendship and affection of [the] people, and because I was convinced that their conversion to our Holy Faith would be better promoted through love than through force, I presented some of them with red caps and some strings of glass beads which they placed around their necks, and with other trifles of insignificant worth that delighted them and by which we have got a wonderful hold on their affections. . . . A man from Conception Island was presented with a red cap and a string of small green glass beads. (Orchard, 1929, p. 14.)

In this simple manner was begun the acculturational process that led ultimately to the disintegration of aboriginal American culture.

It was more than a century later that European glass beads reached the western Great Lakes region, introduced there by Frenchmen. Glass beads were traded to the Indians by the French throughout the seventeenth and much of the eighteenth century. After 1760 the trade in the western Great Lakes area was taken over by the British, and after 1800 the Americans dominated the fur trade in the area. Beads remained in demand, so that both the British and the Americans carried them as media of exchange with the Indians for furs. Thus beads of glass were imported continuously into the western Great Lakes region from about A.D. 1610 until after the War of 1812.

Because glass beads were imported into the region over such a long period and because the styles of beads changed from time to time and because such beads are often present in the graves and sites of former villages of the Indians, it seems reasonable to suppose that beads of glass could be used by archaeologists to date undocumented Indian sites of the historic or contact period.

The idea of a time perspective based on trade beads is an old one. Some twenty-five years ago I thought it would be easy to trace various styles of beads to their European source, find out the date of the manufacture, and produce a sequence of bead styles that could, by association with Indian remains, be used to date these remains. But it has not been easy, even for those scholars specifically trained in historical research. At this writing I do not know of anyone who has successfully traced styles of beads to their sources of manufacture in Europe and obtained documented evidence of the times during which they were made. In fact, I do not know for certain where the beads were manufactured, but I suppose that most of the early ones were made in Venice, or perhaps in Amsterdam by imported artisans (see Van der Sleen, 1963).

Happily there is an easier way to obtain a chronology based on trade beads — a way that makes use of data that were not available twenty-five years ago. Within the last quarter of a century various historically documented sites that contained trade beads have been excavated by archaeologists. Specific sites or clusters of sites were occupied during limited and known periods of time; therefore the glass beads associated with these sites can be dated in a general way. Assemblages of beads from dated sites can be arranged in chronological order and studied comparatively to determine the types of beads that seem to be diagnostic of a given segment of time. The bead chronology thus constructed can then be used in the dating of undocumented sites encountered by the archaeologists who are interested in the historic period.

BEADS OF THE EARLY HISTORIC PERIOD

In the western Great Lakes region the earliest sites that have contained glass beads were those of the Huron and related Iroquoian-speaking groups that lived in Ontario near Georgian Bay, Lake Simcoe, and Lake Huron. And in this former land of Huronia there are two scientifically excavated sites that contained glass beads. Each of these sites is well documented historically. The first is that of the Jesuit mission, Sainte Marie I, that existed from A.D. 1639 to 1649 (see Kidd, 1949). The second is the site of the ossuary made at Ossossane in 1636 (see Kidd, 1953). The glass beads from Sainte Marie I and the Ossossane ossuary are listed in Appendix 1.

In addition to the two specific sites just mentioned, there are in Ontario a number of Huron, Petun, and Neutral sites that have produced glass beads. There is good documentary evidence showing that these groups of Indians occupied known areas of Ontario from the time of the arrival of the French, *circa* 1615, until 1650, by which date these Indians had been defeated and dispersed by Iroquois invaders (see Kinietz, 1940, pp. 1–3). Therefore the glass beads associated with Huron, Petun or Tobacco Huron, and Neutral remains in sites confined to the parts of Ontario abandoned by these Indians *circa* 1650 are trade beads representative of the period from about 1600 to 1650. If the beads belonged to a later period they could not have been found in these sites. A number of glass beads from such sites are in the collections of the Royal Ontario Museum at Toronto. A descriptive list of typical beads from Huron and Petun sites is provided in Appendix 2; and glass beads found in a Neutral site in 1837 and described and illustrated by Henry R. Schoolcraft (1853) are listed in Appendix 3.

Considered as a group, the glass beads diagnostic of the Early Historic period are large tubular or bugle beads, star or chevron beads, and beads with vertical stripes of two colors (Fig. 16). Tubular or bugle beads range from ½ inch to more than 2 inches in length and may be round, square, or triangular in cross section. Some beads which are square in section may be twisted, and some of the beads with round sections are fluted. Usual colors are dull brick-red or blue. Some of the bugle beads with round sections are blue with vertical (parallel to line hole) white stripes. A common style of polychrome bead is round, oval, or spheroidal, up to ½ inch in length, and dull brick-red in color, with inlaid white stripes, in each of which is centered a blue stripe. However, the queen of Early Historic period beads is the chevron or star bead. These are round, spheroidal, or barrel-shaped and frequently of large size, from ½ to 1½ inches long (Fig. 16, top row). The chevron or star beads are made of six or more concentric layers of colored glass. Alternate layers of deep blue, brick-red, white, and sometimes other colors were used. The main layers of glass were separated by thinner layers worked into a series of zigzags. When the ends of these beads were ground into curved surfaces the colored bands produced a star or chevron-like pattern, and grinding the sides of these beads produced alternate stripes of different colors. These beads and those described above are often associated with various colors of monochrome beads of

Fig. 16. — Glass beads diagnostic of the Early Historic period, 1610–1670. Beads are from various sites in Ontario. Courtesy of Chicago Natural History Museum.

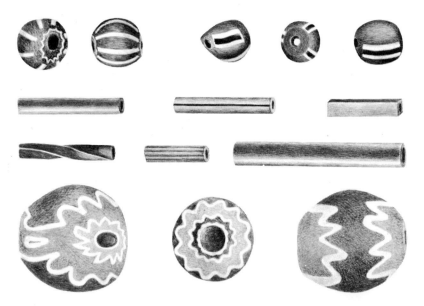

spheroidal shape. There are also a few spheroidal polychrome beads with spiral stripes, but they are a minority style. However, polychrome beads with spiral stripes appear in abundance in the Middle Historic period, for which they are diagnostic types.

BEADS OF THE MIDDLE HISTORIC PERIOD

There are four historically documented sites that have provided excellent data on the glass beads of the Middle Historic period, 1670 to 1760. Two of these sites are in the western Great Lakes region, one is in the lower Mississippi Valley, and one is in the James Bay area. Old Fort Albany, a trading establishment on the west coast of James Bay close to the mouth of the Albany River, was built in 1680 by the Hudson's Bay Company and was destroyed in 1715. The ruins of this fort were excavated by Walter A. Kenyon of the Royal Ontario Museum, who kindly allowed me to examine the glass beads recovered from the site. This collection of beads is listed and described in Appendix 4.

The historically documented site that has produced glass beads in the lower Mississippi Valley is the Fatherland site in Natchez, Mississippi. This site was once the "Grand Village" of the Natchez Indians (Ford, 1936, pp. 50–53), and was occupied from sometime before 1682 until 1730. Although the Natchez were visited by the French as early as 1682 the period of intensive contact did not begin until about 1700, and it ended in 1730 when the French defeated the Natchez in war and drove them from the area. Excavations at the Fatherland site (Ford, 1936, pp. 59–64) produced quantities of glass beads in association with other French trade objects and artifacts of native manufacture. The glass beads from the Fatherland site are thus indicative of styles in use by the French between 1682 and 1730. In 1940, I made analyses of collections of glass beads from the Fatherland site and noted their similarities to glass beads from the Fort St. Joseph area in Michigan (Quimby, 1942, pp. 545–46, and Plate I, Figs. 1–18), and reached the conclusion that the glass beads traded by the French in the lower Mississippi Valley were identical to those traded by the French in the western Great Lakes region.

Fort St. Joseph, in the vicinity of present-day Niles, Michigan, was established shortly before 1700 and lasted until 1781, although its heyday as a trading establishment was from about 1700 to 1763 (see Ballard, 1949). In 1937, I studied the collections of glass trade beads from Fort St. Joseph and vicinity in the Historical Museum at Niles. In 1961, I re-examined these beads and took photographs in color of some of them. A list of the styles of glass beads found at the Fatherland site and in the vicinity of Fort St. Joseph is provided in Appendix 5.

The glass beads from the Fatherland site in Mississippi and the Fort St. Joseph area in southwestern Michigan are identical to the beads found at the site of Fort Michilimackinac at Mackinaw City in northern Michigan (see Maxwell and Binford, 1961, pp. 89, 90, and 117). Fort Michilimackinac was occupied by the French in the second half of the Middle Historic period. I have examined a number of the beads found during the excavation of the site as well as beads in two private collections obtained from the site many years earlier. One bead type found at Fort Michilimackinac and not at Fort St. Joseph or the Fatherland site consisted of a bright blue glass disk about $\frac{3}{16}$ inch thick and about $\frac{3}{4}$ inch in diameter. It had an inlaid design in white of a man-in-the-moon on the obverse and a comet with two stars on the reverse. This type of bead has also been found associated with other types of beads representative of the Middle Historic period in an Indian grave on Old Birch Island in northern Georgian Bay (see Greenman, 1951, pp. 28, 29, and 55). Thus the man-in-the-moon bead, although of rare occurrence, seems to be a diagnostic type of the Middle Historic period.

Taken as a group, the polychrome beads diagnostic of the Middle Historic period (Fig. 17) are spheroidal or elongate spheroidal beads ranging from $\frac{3}{8}$ to $\frac{3}{4}$ inch in length and $\frac{1}{8}$ to $\frac{1}{2}$ inch in diameter, with straight or spiral stripes in a single contrasting color. These spiral stripes are relatively more abundant than the straight stripes in this period. Of monochrome beads (Fig. 17) similarly considered, the diagnostic forms are elongate spheroids, decahedrals with eight facets and two flat ends, raspberry (or mulberry) forms, egg-shaped (wire-wound) forms, usually quite large, and spheroidal beads with fluting. Such monochrome beads, other than seed beads used to decorate clothing and bags, ranged in length from $\frac{1}{4}$ to $1\frac{1}{8}$ inches and in diameter from $\frac{1}{8}$ to $\frac{5}{8}$ inch.

Although there is undoubtedly some overlap in bead styles between the Early and Middle Historic periods, the chevron or star bead of the early period is lacking in the middle period. Conversely, the spheroidal or elongate spheroidal beads with spiral stripes and the egg-shaped wire-wound beads of the Middle Historic period do not occur in the Early Historic period. But some Middle Historic period bead styles may also represent the closing years of the Early Historic period.

BEADS OF THE LATE HISTORIC PERIOD

Fortunately, the glass beads representative of the Late Historic period are quite different from those of the Early and Middle Historic periods and therefore fairly easy to recognize. Moreover, they have been found repeatedly in direct association with the kinds of silver ornaments made for the fur trade between 1760 and 1820, and thus they clearly belong to the Late Historic period (see Herrick, 1958).

Except for the small (seed) beads used in beadwork of various kinds there seem to be relatively fewer types of beads used in the Late Historic period. Polychrome beads particularly appear to be rare. One style of polychrome bead that is diagnostic of the Late

Fig. 17. — Glass beads representative of the Middle Historic period, 1670–1760. Courtesy of Chicago Natural History Museum.

Historic period consists of oval or barrel-shaped (wire-wound) beads of blue or green translucent glass with wreaths of leaves in yellow or white enamel encircling the mid-sections (equators). Another polychrome bead that is representative of the Late Historic period belongs to the polka dot or eyed bead class. It is round or spheroidal, usually about ⅜ inch in diameter, and made of opaque glass that is dark blue or black. The dots, or eyes, are enamel and the colors vary. Some dots are white. Others are white partly superimposed by yellow, and still others have alternately red and blue dots on top of the white. However, polychrome beads of any sort are rare in the Late Historic period and therefore not as useful for dating purposes as some other types of beads.

A more popular class of monochrome beads diagnostic of the Late Historic period embraces several sizes and colors of multifaceted cut glass forms (Fig. 18). Some varieties of this class are about ¼ inch in diameter and ¼ to ½ inch long, with eighteen or more facets. Colors noted are aquamarine blue, emerald green, crystal, and old heliotrope or lavender. Some smaller varieties of multifaceted beads of cut glass are ³⁄₁₆ inch in diameter and from ³⁄₁₆ to ⁵⁄₁₆ inch in length. They have fifteen or more facets and generally are cobalt blue although some are of crystal color. Most of the multifaceted varieties of beads are translucent regardless of color. And all of the varieties of multifaceted cut glass beads, regardless of color and size, are diagnostic of the Late Historic period.

Imitation wampum beads in opaque white, black, or dark blue are also characteristic of the late period. They are small tubular beads about ⅛ inch in diameter and ³⁄₁₆ to ⁵⁄₁₆ inch in length. It is often difficult for me to distinguish these beads from the manufactured shell beads or wampum that also were traded by white men during the same period.

Other characteristic styles of glass monochrome beads include the following: oblate spheroidal beads of opaque dirty pink ranging from ³⁄₁₆ to ⅜ inch in diameter and from ⅛ to ¼ inch in length; spheroidal and oblate spheroidal beads of translucent green or blue from ¼ to ⅜ inch in diameter; spheroidal and drawn teardrop forms of opaque glossy black about ¼ to ⅜ inch in diameter; oblate spheroidal beads of translucent light blue ³⁄₁₆ inch in diameter; spheroidal beads of translucent blue ³⁄₁₆ to ¼ inch in diameter; and spheroidal beads of apple red over a pinkish core ranging in diameter from ³⁄₁₆ to ⁵⁄₁₆ inch.

In general, glass beads are not so important in dating sites of the Late Historic period as they are in the Early and Middle Historic periods. This is because of the popularity of silver ornaments in the late period. Whereas glass beads were the most popular form of imported adornment in the Early and Middle Historic periods they are relegated to a secondary position or practically superseded by various kinds of silver ornaments in the Late Historic period. However, seed beads — small beads used in ornamental bead work rather than in necklaces (see Fig. 19) — became

Fig. 18. — Glass beads representative of the Late Historic period, 1760–1820. Courtesy of Chicago Natural History Museum.

Fig. 19. — Small glass beads, called seed beads, woven into an ornamental pattern on garters made about 1760. These garters are in the collection of Chicago Natural History Museum. The upper two garters were acquired by Jeffrey Amherst between 1758 and 1763.

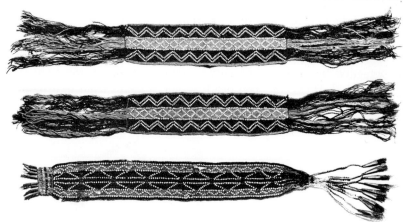

relatively more popular and more abundant in the Late Historic period. And although seed beads deserve better treatment than I have given them, their chronological importance is negligible compared to that of trade silver ornaments, which are discussed in Chapter 7.

REFERENCES

Ballard, 1949; Ford, 1936; Greenman, 1951; Herrick, 1958; Kidd, 1949, 1953; Kinietz, 1940; Maxwell and Binford, 1961; Orchard, 1929; Quimby, 1942; Schoolcraft, 1853; Van der Sleen, 1963.

CHAPTER 7

THE TIME OF THE TRADE SILVER

The best single criterion for dating archaeological sites of the Late Historic period, 1760 to 1820, is the presence of silver ornaments of kinds made for use in the fur trade by silversmiths in Canada, England, and the United States. Such ornaments were not used in the western Great Lakes fur trade before 1760, but became very popular soon after that date. For instance, in June of 1763, when Alexander Henry, the well-known fur trader, was captured by Chippewa Indians at Fort Michilimackinac, he had for sale a large quantity of "silver armbands, and other valuable ornaments" which were taken from him, along with other trade goods (Henry, ed. Bain, 1901, p. 76).

Silver ornaments can be dated in two ways. Those made in London were stamped not only with the initials of the silversmith who made them but also with hallmarks and a date letter that changed every fiscal year (Fig. 21, A, K, and P). Thus, by learning the London system of hallmarks and date letters, one may determine the year of manufacture for a given silver ornament. American and Canadian silversmiths were not governed by such an accommodating system. Although they frequently stamped their initials on their products, they did not use hallmarks and date letters.

However, it is possible to find out the years during which given Canadian or American silversmiths practiced their trade and thus date their works in a general way. For instance, it might be known that a certain Canadian silversmith worked between the years 1779 and 1806, and thus any silver ornament with his particular mark would date from 1779 to 1806, and could not be earlier than 1779, although it could be later than 1806.

The most common types of ornaments were gorgets, brooches, crosses, armbands, wristbands, and earbobs. Less common were earwheels, hair pipes, hair plates, animal effigies, lockets, hat bands and crowns, and cradle-board decorations.

Wristbands were C-shaped bracelets made of sheet silver. Some of them were quite plain whereas others were ridged or had scalloped edges. Engraved decorations were rare. Wristbands frequently were stamped with the mark of the silversmith who made them. These ornaments were worn generally by women, but sometimes by men, especially in the first half of the Late Historic period.

Armbands were rather wide strips of sheet silver curved into a C-shape to fit a man's arm above the elbow (see Fig. 32). Some armbands were engraved with a central design or symbol and often bordered by longitudinal ridges, but others were plain. Both styles were perforated at the ends for the insertion of cords or thongs by which the armband was held and adjusted to the size of the wearer's arm.

Gorgets, which were chest ornaments worn by men, were of two kinds. The crescent-shaped gorget, or half moon, was concavo-convex in section and either plain or engraved upon the convex side. Suspension holes, often equipped with bosses or buttons, were provided at the points of the crescent. The engraved designs were similar to those placed on armbands. The crescent-shaped gorget as used by the Indians was an adaptation of the gorget worn by British army officers as a badge of rank, and the earliest silver gorgets worn by Indians probably were actual officers' gorgets. The British commissioned Indian leaders as "gorget captains" and presented them with silver gorgets and armbands engraved with the royal arms (Woodward, 1945).

The round gorget or moon was circular in outline and concavo-convex in section. The engraved decoration occurs on the concave side. Two suspension holes frequently were equipped with hollow bosses. The round gorget probably had its origin in the aboriginal shell gorget of the Indians, and the degree of correspondence between the native shell gorget and the introduced silver form is impressive. Both have the same basic shape — round with a concavo-convex section. Moreover, both were engraved on the concave face of the gorget and both had suspension holes in the same positions.

Several kinds of brooches, all of European origin, were manufactured for the Indian trade. They came originally from Scotland and England (Parker, 1910, p. 353), and possibly from Germany (Woodward, 1945, p. 331). Although brooches at first were worn by Indian men as well as women, they came to be particularly favored by women. Among the known varieties of brooches were the following:

(1) Circular ornate or pierced brooches were concavo-convex disks with central, circular openings across which lay a hinged pin for fastening the brooch to the garment. These brooches were ornamented with a symmetrical arrangement of oval, triangular, diamond-shaped, and semilunar perforations (Fig. 20, *lower left*). In some instances engraved geometric designs were added to the solid parts of the convex face of the brooch.

(2) Plain circular brooches were similar in many ways to the circular ornate brooches, but lacked the cut perforations. However, plain circular brooches were sometimes engraved with simple geometric design. Miniature round brooches were manufactured and traded by the thousands. They were simple rings of silver, empty in the middle except for silver cross-pins to fasten them to garments. They were often worn in groups to produce a massed effect reminiscent of chain mail or flexible armor.

(3) Star brooches were multipointed, were concavo-convex in section, and had a round opening in the center. The various points of the star were sometimes enclosed with a rim or narrow band (Fig. 20, *lower left*). Some other styles of small brooches in common use were quadrilateral brooches, heart and crowned-heart brooches, double heart and crowned double heart brooches, and Masonic brooches.

There were several varieties of silver ear ornaments, including earrings, earbobs, and ear wheels. Ear wheels were flat disks punched or cut out in various patterns so that the perforations left a tracing of geometric design enclosed within a circular rim.

Hair plates were disks that were concavo-convex in section. They seem to have been somewhat similar to brooches, but were worn as hair ornaments and also used, in later years at least, to decorate pendent strips of fur or braided hair. Although they are mentioned in early trade inventories and orders, actual specimens seem to be rare in collections of early trade silver. Possibly hair plates have been mistakenly identified as brooches.

Fig. 20. — Typical ornaments of silver used in the fur trade during the Late Historic period, 1760–1820. Courtesy of Chicago Natural History Museum. *Upper left:* beaver effigy pendants, composite pendant with engraved figure, single- and double-barred crosses, from Round Island, Michigan. *Lower left:* brooches, from Great Lakes region. *Right:* large cross, from Cross Village, Michigan.

Hair pipes were silver tubes worn as hair ornaments by men and perhaps by women. Silver crowns, headbands, or hatbands were made of sheet silver and often engraved and perforated to produce geometric designs. These ornaments were worn by men. Miscellaneous silver ornaments that appear to have been made in limited quantities were such items as elaborate cradle-board ornaments (Barbeau, 1942, p. 14), spoon-shaped lockets (Quimby, 1937, pp. 17–18, and Fig. 2), and hollow pendants in the form of animals such as bear and beaver. Beaver-shaped pendants (Fig. 20, *upper left*) were made by Robert Cruickshank of Montreal, a well-known Canadian silversmith. Cruickshank's silver beavers probably were made initially at the request of Indians from the northern half of the western Great Lakes region, for it was in this area that the beaver effigy pendant made of stone had a respectable antiquity. For instance, the prehistoric levels of a Chippewa site on the north shore of Lake Superior produced a nicely carved beaver effigy of gray dense stone, and beaver effigy pendants made of catlinite have been recovered from Middle Historic period sites along the northern shore of Lake Michigan.

Silver crosses of several kinds were common ornaments used in the Indian trade. They were worn by the men as chest ornaments or sometimes as ear ornaments. Gillingham (1943, p. 86) shows an old painting of an Indian adorned with silver ornaments including a double-barred cross hanging from each ear. Silver crosses ranged in size from miniature ones about an inch in length to large crosses 12 inches long. Both single-barred crosses and double-barred crosses (Fig. 20, *upper left*) were in general use. Moreover, both kinds of crosses were in some instances extremely elaborate (Fig. 20, *right*). Crosses were sometimes embellished with engravings of scrolls and conventionalized floral forms.

It was once popularly believed that these single- and double-barred crosses of silver had been given to Christian converts among the Indians by seventeenth-century missionaries. It was also once believed that the initials "CA" stamped on some crosses stood for "Cardinal Archbishop" or Father "Claude Allouez," and the initials "RC" stamped on other crosses stood for "Richelieu Cardinal." It is, of course, now known that "CA" was the maker's stamp of Charles Arnoldi of Montreal and that "RC" was the maker's mark of Robert Cruickshank of Montreal. Between 1780 and 1800 these two silversmiths must have made hundreds of crosses bearing their marks. It is probable that thousands of crosses were manufactured for the fur trade by various silversmiths, and it seems certain that they were made for and used as ornaments rather than as religious symbols.

As previously mentioned, silver gorgets and armbands often were engraved with pictorial representations of real or mythical animals, human beings, official arms of Great Britain and the United States, flowers or other plants, and various scenes. In Figure 20, *upper left*, there is illustrated a composite pendant made from a silver armband upon which was engraved a conventionalized representation of an Indian. And in Figure 29 there are shown some examples of the real and mythical animals engraved on silver armbands and gorgets. An example of the "scene" type of engraving appears in Gillingham (1936, frontispiece). This engraving on a gorget made by Joseph Richardson, Jr., of Philadelphia shows an Indian and a white man. The white man, sitting beneath a tree (the tree of peace?) is passing a winged pipe (peace pipe) to the Indian. A fire is burning in the background, and above them is the shining sun. A somewhat frivolous scene described by Woodward (1945, p. 331) consisted of an Indian seated on a keg of rum and drinking from a bottle. This engraving appeared on a very large silver cross, an unusual circumstance, as crosses generally were not decorated with representational engravings. In an order for silver ornaments sent from Albany Factory, a Hudson's Bay Company fur trading post in Canada, to England in 1796, there is a description of the scene desired: "Gorgets, with the following engravings. Vizt. to represent Albany (fort), two or three Houses, some Indian Tents and Indian Men & Women" (Barbeau, 1940, p. 37). Silver gorgets and armbands issued to the Indians by agents of England or the United States were usually engraved with the official arms of those countries. Entries in the ledgers of the Philadelphia silversmith Joseph Richardson, Jr., show that in 1798 he decorated silver ornaments with engravings of eagles and the arms of the United States. These silver ornaments had been ordered from him by the purveyor for the federal government (Gillingham, 1943, pp. 88–89), and probably were intended for official presentations. Official inventories of silver ornaments used by the British (see Quimby, 1937, p. 20) show that the "King's arms and supporters" were engraved on arm-bands and gorgets.

The floral motifs engraved on some gorgets and armbands prob-ably were an expression of the general Algonkian use of floral patterns which, regardless of ultimate origin, was well estab-lished in the time of the trade silver. The mythical animals (see Fig. 29, D and L) probably were expressions of the religious be-liefs of Algonkian-speaking Indians. However, the real animals depicted in engravings on silver probably were clan or personal symbols. Possibly the Indians made drawings of the animals for the trader, who in turn submitted them to the silversmith for en-graving, or in some cases it may have been the trader who actu-ally engraved the ornaments. It is interesting to note the similarity in style between some of the animals engraved on silver orna-ments and some of those inscribed on birch bark or drawn on paper as signatures to treaties by Indians of the western Great Lakes region (Fig. 29, G and K), whereas other engravings of ani-mals on silver seem to represent traditional European styles of depiction (Fig. 29, C). The differences in style may indicate whether or not the engraver was copying samples submitted by Indian customers. Probably the mythical animals had to be drawn or described first by Indians so that they could be engraved on silver by the trader or silversmith.

The white men who made the ornaments for trade with Indians were generally well-known silversmiths who were working in Eng-land, Canada, or the United States (see hallmarks in Fig. 21). For a listing of such silversmiths and the identifying marks they stamped on their silver see Appendix 6. These silversmiths were well paid for their work, because only ornaments of good quality of silver and craftsmanship were acceptable for use in the fur trade. For instance, in May of 1759, Philip Syng of Philadelphia was paid 35 pounds and 2 shillings for 12 armbands, 12 dozen brooches, 11 dozen crosses, and 24 hair plates. In the same year during July and August, Joseph Richardson (the elder) was paid more than 115 pounds for 720 ornaments (Gillingham, 1936, pp. 12–13). These ornaments, however, were being made for trade with eastern Indians and did not reach the western Great Lakes

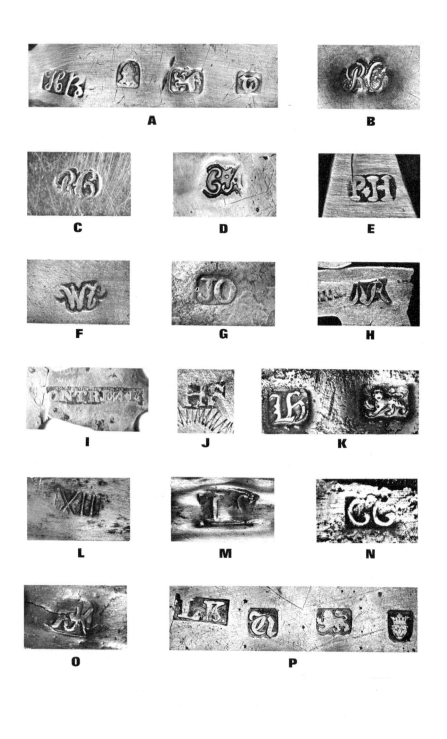

Fig. 21. (facing page). — Marks of silversmiths stamped on silver ornaments made for the fur trade in the Late Historic period, 1760–1820. Courtesy of Chicago Natural History Museum. A, Hester Bateman; B, C, Robert Cruickshank; D, Charles Arnoldi; E, Pierre Huguet dit Latour; F, unidentified, probably Canadian; G, John Oakes; H, Narcisse Roy; I, J, unidentified Montreal smiths; K, unidentified British; L, unidentified, probably Canadian; M, Jonas Schindler or the Widow Schindler; N, Christian Grothe; O, John Kinzie; P, Luke Kendall. (Not all identifications are positive.)

region until after 1760. Between May 1759 and May 1763 more than 8,000 silver ornaments were made by three Philadelphia silversmiths — Hollingshead, Richardson (the elder), and Syng — who collectively received for them a sum of more than 2,800 pounds (Gillingham, 1936, p. 25).

Excerpts from the journal of accounts of James and Andrew McGill as quoted by Traquair (1938, p. 5) show that the McGill Company spent upwards of 4,184 pounds for silver ornaments between August 1797 and April 1801. The Canadian silversmiths to whom this money was paid were Curtius, Pierre Huguet dit Latour, the Widow Schindler, and Robert Cruickshank. Single payments to Pierre Huguet dit Latour for silver ornaments ran as high as 773 pounds, 10 shillings, and 11 deniers. In 1779 and 1780 Col. Guy Johnson charged the Crown about 550 pounds for purchases of silver ornaments for distribution among the Indians. The silver ornaments consisted of gorgets, armbands, brooches, and earbobs (Barbeau, 1940, p. 34). Gillingham (1943, p. 89) reproduces a bill for silver ornaments rendered by Joseph Richardson, Jr., of Philadelphia on April 4, 1798, which shows that Richardson made, and in some cases engraved, 1,926 silver ornaments weighing more than 310 ounces, for which he charged a total of 323 pounds, 2 shillings, and 8.5 cents.

In 1801, Narcisse Roy, a Canadian silversmith, received 342 pounds in payment for about 9,000 silver ornaments. In the same year Robert Cruickshank, another Canadian silversmith, received a single payment of 318 pounds for a somewhat similar order of silver ornaments (Barbeau, 1940, p. 31). And in 1808, Augustin Lagrave of Sandwich, Ontario, was paid about 31 pounds for making 4,792 small (miniature round) brooches at 5 shillings per hundred, 15 large brooches at 2 shillings each, 13 ear wheels at 2 shillings each, and 12 large earwheels at 2 shillings each (McDonald, 1939). In the same year Pierre Riople of Sandwich was paid about 29 pounds for "polishing" 600 brooches, 1,700 small brooches, 125 pairs of earbobs, 36 small wristbands, 6 armbands, 23 "half moons" (crescent-shaped gorgets), 4 "moons" (circular gorgets), 1 headband, 3 crosses, 6 small crosses, 40 "Emb's" brooches, 78 ear wheels, 7 "wings," and 300 pairs of earbobs (McDonald, 1939). During 1820 and 1821 the United States Government paid $604.15 to Charles A. Burnett, then of Georgetown, D.C., for the manufacture of armbands, gorgets, brooches, and other ornaments for distribution among the Indians (Gillingham, 1938). From Chauncey S. Payne of Detroit the United States Government purchased silver ornaments for distribution to the Indians at Sault Ste Marie, Mackinac, and L'Arbre Croche in 1820. Payne was paid $1,402.51 for 85 gorgets, 82 armbands, 336 brooches, 103 ear wheels, 3,800 small brooches, 66 wristbands, and 600 earbobs (Gillingham, 1938, personal communication).

Silver ornaments manufactured by white silversmiths were a universal element in the culture of Indians living in the western Great Lakes region during the Late Historic period, 1760 to 1820 or later. As pointed out to me by Dr. David Baerreis (personal communication, 1963), these silver ornaments regardless of their European origins were uniquely Indian in their cultural context in the New World. They were made for Indians and were used by Indians and, what is most important, they were buried with deceased Indians. Moreover, these silver ornaments can be dated not only to the Late Historic period in general but also to temporal segments within the period. If an unmarked circular gorget is found in a grave, I know that the grave has a date somewhere in the Late Historic period, after 1760, while if the grave contains a silver armband made by Hester Bateman of London and it has the proper year mark, I would know that the burial could not have been made before 1779. Thus, quite apart from any other cultural meaning these ornaments may have, they are ideal chronological indicators for the Late Historic period, or parts thereof.

REFERENCES

Barbeau, 1940, 1942; Gillingham, 1936, 1943; Henry, ed. Bain, 1901; McDonald, 1939; Parker, 1910; Quimby, 1937; Traquair, 1938; Woodward, 1945.

CHAPTER 8

THE ARCHAEOLOGY OF THE EARLY
HISTORIC PERIOD, 1610–1670

HURONIA AND VICINITY

Within the western or upper Great Lakes region most of the archaeological sites of the Early Historic period are located on the eastern periphery in the Canadian lands adjacent to Lake Huron and Georgian Bay. Much of this area was fertile, gently rolling land, largely forested with deciduous trees. In the lands between Lake Simcoe and Georgian Bay there lived the Hurons, and westward of them there lived similar Indians called the Tobacco Hurons or Petuns. Both groups of Indians spoke Iroquoian languages, dwelt in palisaded villages, and obtained their food principally by agriculture. In the cleared fields beside their towns these Indians raised corn, beans, pumpkins or squashes, sunflowers, and tobacco — crops that even to this day are raised in the same area by modern Canadian farmers. The combined Huron-Petun population has been estimated at 45,000 to 60,000 persons, but whatever the actual figure, this certainly was the largest concentration of Indians in the western Great Lakes region.

Of Hurons and Petuns the former seem to have been the largest group. The probable population of Huronia was at least 30,000 souls (see Popham, 1950, p. 86). And the largest Huron town in seventeenth-century Huronia was Cahiague, with a population of 4,000 to 6,000 men, women, and children. According to ethnohistorical sources Cahiague was a palisaded town containing two hundred long-houses. Except for some large towns in western Huronia all other Huron villages were one-half or one-quarter the size of Cahiague. Samuel de Champlain visited Cahiague in the summer of 1615. About 350 years later, in the summer of 1964, I visited the site of Cahiague and witnessed the archaeological excavations of a field party working for the University of Toronto under the direction of Dr. J. Norman Emerson, professor of anthropology and archaeology at the University.

The Cahiague site occupies an area of 25 acres on a tract of land near Warminster in Simcoe County, Ontario. There, under the supervision of Professor Emerson, students are carefully uncovering the remains of seventeenth-century Cahiague. The positions and sizes of former houses are manifested by stained molds or rotted post fragments in the soil of the sites. These large houses were bunched together with their entrances facing each other. The typical Huron dwelling was a long rectangular structure with a rounded roof. It was made of a pole framework covered with large slabs or sheets of elm bark. According to Professor Emerson, "Huron houses seem to have been constructed in multiples of about thirty feet, and lengths of ninety, one-hundred and twenty, one hundred and fifty, and even one hundred and eighty have been excavated" (Emerson, 1961, VII, 2). The usual long-house, about 30 by 120 feet, contained some 3,600 square feet of living space. In such a house there lived twenty-three to twenty-five men, women, and children comprising four or five families related to each other through the female lineage.

The outer wall of the Huron long-house, according to Dr. Emerson, was constructed of poles 3 to 4 inches in diameter and set 2 feet 6 inches into the ground. These poles were arranged in pairs, inner and outer poles, 6 inches apart. The paired poles were placed at intervals of 18 inches. Slabs of elm bark were lashed between the paired poles of the outer wall, then these poles were bent over and joined at the top to make a rounded roof. One end of the house was squared and had a doorway and a protective vestibule. The opposite end of the house was rounded and used as a storage room for corn. It was separated from the rest of the house by a straight partition supported by posts. Inside the rest of the house there was a long central corridor, on each side of which were sleeping benches partitioned into cubicles about 10 feet square. In the central corridor there were fireplaces and usually some large support posts about 10 inches in diameter. There were generally two, but sometimes four or more, large fireplaces. Numerous small post holes ½ to 1½ inches in diameter at the ends of these hearths suggest pot-holders and roasting sticks. Smaller hearths and rectangular storage pits were situated haphazardly over the floor of the long-house.

In addition to the doorway at the squared end of the long-house there usually was another entrance on the side protected from the wind. Through these doors passed not only the Huron occupants of the long-house but also their refuse. At the Cahiague site, according to Dr. Emerson, the houses were cleaned periodically and the refuse was swept out through both doors. We know that this was the case for the following reasons: First of all, there was hardly any debris found on the floors of excavated long-houses, a fact that indicates cleaning. Secondly, there were middens or refuse dumps located outside but near the doors of the long-houses and in these dumps were the refuse and broken tools, lost ornaments, etc., that one would otherwise expect to find on the long-house floors. Moreover, the refuse piles were layered in a manner indicative of periodic accumulation. And finally, there were instances in which fragments of pottery from a midden by one door of a long-house would fit together with fragments found in another midden by the other door of the long-house.

Pottery was exceedingly abundant among the Huron. From ethnohistorical records we know that the women made the pottery. We also know that at any given time there were three generations of closely related women in a given long-house. Moreover, at marriage, a girl did not leave the long-house and her female relations. Instead her husband joined her. Under conditions such as these, there was unusual stability and adherence to tradition in the manufactures and handicrafts of the Huron women. And this stability and rigidity of tradition is reflected in the Huron pottery excavated by archaeologists.

Huron pottery of the Early Historic period (Fig. 22) consisted

of globular jars with round bottoms, constricted necks, and slightly flaring rims with relatively narrow collars and flat lips. Decoration, largely confined to the collar, was produced by incising while the clay was still plastic. Patterns of closely spaced vertical, horizontal, or oblique lines or a simple combination of alternating areas of such lines encircled the collared portion of the rim. Sometimes the pattern was embellished by a row of punctate impressions encircling the rim just beneath the collar. This simple decorative style was the most common among the Huron of the Early Historic period. Some jars had more elaborate designs, higher collars, decoration on shoulder area as well as collar, loop handles attached to the rim, castellations of the rim, or a combination of these attributes, but such vessels were not the common ware.

Huron pottery of the Early Historic period was made by the paddle and anvil method. Professor Emerson (1961, VI, 2) describes this method as follows: "A ball of clay was worked and kneaded. A concavity was gradually worked into the centre of it and expanded. A flat rounded stone was inserted and the outside was paddled, gradually thinning and shaping the vessel. Clay was added and gradually the neck and collar areas were formed." The vessel was carefully smoothed all over and then decorated while the clay was still plastic. And after sufficient drying the vessel was hardened in the flames of burning wood in an open fire. The firing of the pottery produced reddish, orange, or drab brown colors, depending on the temperature of the fire, the impurities contained in the clay, and the amount of air reaching the vessel. According to Dr. Emerson, historic Huron sites produce a rather high percentage of black wares which are the result of a technique of secondary firing at low temperatures.

In general the pottery of the Huron was well and skillfully made. The clay, which contained small particles of granitic stone, was well mixed and of even texture when fired. Vessel walls were of uniform thickness and the vessels were of uniform size, most of them approximately 12 inches high and 8 or 9 inches in diameter at the top. Such uniformity of technique, form, decoration, and size indicates that the Huron potter had a firm conceptualization of the finished product before she made the pot. Moreover, she was subject to the approval and criticism of the older generations of women from whom she had learned her craft.

In addition to pottery, household equipment consisted of woven mats, wooden bowls and ladles, various sizes of boxes and containers made of bark, bedding made of animal skins and furs, thin, double-pointed needles or bodkins of bone with center holes, and a number of things obtained from the French. These included woolen blankets, brass kettles, iron axes, and knives, awls, and needles of iron.

Huron arrowheads from Cahiague and other sites were triangular in outline, usually about 1½ inches long, and made of chipped chert or flint. These had straight or slightly convex sides and straight or slightly concave bases. The Huron Indians also used iron arrowheads as well as iron knives, awls, and fishhooks. Ornaments consisted of European glass beads of kinds typical of the Early Historic period, brass rings and bracelets, and beads and pendants made of reddish slate or catlinite from the upper Mississippi Valley or white conch shell from the Atlantic Coast. Disk-shaped objects of bone or pottery about 1¼ inches in diameter were used in games of chance.

Huron tobacco pipes were the most elaborate of all in the western Great Lakes region during the historic period (see Ridley, 1952, p. 201). There were various forms of effigy pipes made of clay or stone. Those of stone include a type with a human figure projecting from the rim of the bowl and a style with a lizard or salamander on it. Effigy pipes of fired clay include the following varieties: the pinched face pipe, the blowing face pipe with twisted stem, the owl pipe, crow pipe, bird pipe, bear pipe, and fox or wolf pipe. Another typical variety of Huron pipe of fired clay was characterized by a curved stem decorated with fluting and incising and a bowl with a square rim and four castellations. Another common Huron style consisted of a pipe with a round and cup-shaped bowl that resembles an acorn cup and a curved stem that is round in cross section. The bowl is completely covered with incised annular lines, beneath which there frequently occurs an encircling row of closely space punctate impressions. Less common was a carefully modeled pipe shaped like a bent trumpet with a curved stem and widely flaring and thickened rim on the bowl. The stem of such a pipe was fluted and otherwise decorated, and the bowl was ornamented with vertical incising. Rather simple Huron pipes of stone included a vase-shaped form and a conical form. These were stemless and required the addition of a wooden stem or reed before they could be smoked.

Huron burial practices were spectacular; and since they were observed by the French there are historical accounts to supplement the archaeological evidence. The custom among the Huron Indians was to place their dead in temporary graves during the interim period (eight to twelve years) between the great Feasts of the Dead — an elaborate ceremony, in the course of which all the deceased from each Huron town were removed from their temporary graves and brought together at an ossuary for a mass burial.

In May 1636 the Feast of the Dead was held at the Huron town of Ossossane, and the Jesuit priest Jean de Brébeuf was present. His recorded account of this event is in part as follows (see Kidd, 1953, pp. 372–73):

The feast of the Dead is the most renowned ceremony among the Hurons; they give it the name of feast because, . . . when the bodies are taken from their Cemeteries, each Captain [chief] makes a feast for the souls of his Village. . . . This feast abounds in ceremonies. . . . Twelve years or thereabout having elapsed, the Old Men and Notables of the Country assemble, to deliberate . . . on the time at which the feast shall be held. . . . The decision having been made, as all the bodies are to be transported to the Village where is the common grave, each family sees to its dead, but with a care and affection that cannot be described: if they have dead relatives in any part of the Country, they spare no trouble to go for them; they take them from the [temporary] Cemeteries, bear them on their shoulders, and cover them with the finest robes they have. In each Village, they . . . proceed to the [temporary] Cemetery, where those . . . who take care of the graves, draw the bodies from the tombs in the presence of the relatives, who renew their tears and feel afresh the grief they had on the day of the funeral.

I was present at the spectacle, and willingly invite to it all our servants; for I do not think one could see in the world a more vivid picture or more perfect representation of what Man is. For, after having opened the graves, they display . . . all these corpses . . . long enough for the spectators to learn . . . what they will be some day. The flesh of some is quite gone, and there is only parchment on their bones; in other cases, the bodies look as if they had been dried and smoked, and show scarcely any signs of putrefaction; and in still other cases they are still swarming with worms. . . . finally, after some time they strip them of their flesh, taking off the skin and flesh [by handfuls] which they throw into the fire along with robes and mats in which the bodies were wrapped.

The cleaned bones were in some instances rearticulated and clothed in fine robes and decked with ornaments. In other cases they were simply bundled together in beaver-skin bags, some of which were shaped to suggest human effigies and ornamented with beads and bands of red-dyed fur. After preparing the bodies, the tribesmen carried them on their backs from the village to the spot designated as an ossuary. Ceremony prescribed that this journey be drawn out over two or three days.

Brébeuf described the mass burial place or ossuary near Ossossane in the following manner (see Kidd, 1953, pp. 374–75):

It was about the size of the place Royale at Paris. There was in the middle of it a great pit, about ten feet deep and five brasses [25 feet] wide. All around it was a scaffold, a sort of staging very well made, nine to ten brasses in width, and from nine to ten feet high; above this staging there were a number of poles laid across, and well arranged, with cross-poles to which these packages of souls were hung and bound [Fig. 23]. The whole bodies, as they were to be put in the bottom of the pit, had been the preceding day placed under the scaffold. . . . The whole Company ar-

Fig. 23. — Drawing reconstructing the Huron Feast of the Dead as it might have appeared at Ossossane in 1636. Courtesy of Chicago Natural History Museum.

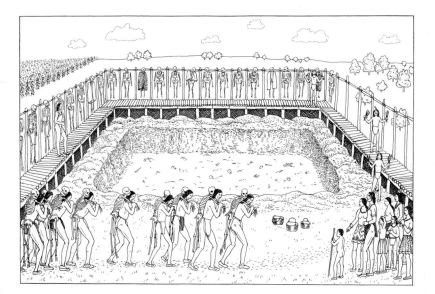

rived with their corpses . . . and divided themselves . . . according to their familes and Villages, and laid on the ground their parcels of souls. . . . They unfolded also their parcels of robes, and all the presents they had brought, and hung them on poles. . . . About three o'clock, each one put away his various articles, and folded up his robes.

Meanwhile, each Captain [chief] gave the signal; and all, at once, loaded with their packages of souls, running as if to the assault of a town, ascended the stage . . . and hung them [the corpses] to the cross poles. . . . About five or six o'clock, they lined the bottom and sides of the pit with fine large new robes, each of ten Beaver skins, in such a way that they extended more than a foot out of it. . . . At seven o'clock, they let down the whole bodies into the pit. . . . On all sides you could have seen them letting down half-decayed bodies . . . ten or twelve [Indians] were in the pit and were arranging the bodies all around it, one after another. They put in the very middle of the pit three large kettles, which could only be of use for souls. . . . I saw very few Porcelain collars [at this time, although] it is true, they put many on the bodies.

All the people passed the night on the spot; they lighted many fires, and slung their kettles. We withdrew for the night . . . with the resolve to return the next morning at daybreak when they were to throw the bones into the pit; but we [were almost late] on account of an accident that happened. One of the souls, which was not securely tied, or was perhaps too heavy for the cord that fastened it, fell of itself into the pit; the noise awakened the Company, who immediately ran and mounted in a crowd upon the scaffold, and emptied indiscriminately each package [of bones] into the pit, keeping, however, the robes in which they were enveloped. . . . As we drew near, we saw nothing less than a picture of Hell. The large space was quite full of fires and flames, and the air resounded in all directions with the confused voices of these Barbarians; the noise ceased . . . and they began to sing. . . .

Nearly all the souls were thrown in when we arrived, for it was done almost at the turning of a hand; each one had made haste, thinking there would not be room enough for all the souls; we saw, however, enough of it to judge the rest. There were five or six in the pit, arranging the bones with poles. The pit was full, within about two feet; they turned back over the bones the robes which bordered the edge of the pit, and covered the remaining space with mats and bark. Then they heaped the pit with sand, poles, and wooden stakes, which they threw in without order. Some women brought to it some dishes of corn; and . . . several Cabins of the Village [Ossossane] provided nets quite full of it, which were thrown upon the pit.

Some three hundred and ten years after the events described by Father Brébeuf the great burial pit near Ossossane was excavated for the Royal Ontario Museum of Archaeology by Kenneth E. Kidd. He found the skeletal remains of about 1,000 persons piled into the pit as described by Brébeuf. "Long bones, for instance, lay in all positions and at all angles; a single femur standing on end might traverse five levels, while crania occupied at least two or or three levels" (Kidd, 1953, p. 359). Surrounding the burial pit, which was about the size stated by Brébeuf, there were molds and soil discolorations manifesting former wooden posts from 6 to 12 inches in diameter. These were the remains of the scaffolding described by Brébeuf. Artifacts found with the bones in the ossuary were relics of the grave offerings made at the ceremony in 1636. These included a large conch shell, over a thousand shell beads of cylindrical shape, many tubular and discoidal beads of shell, triangular and crescentic pendants of shell, a bone pendant carved to represent a human face, some triangular arrowheads of chipped flint, a vase-shaped pipe bowl of polished green stone, reddish slate beads of tubular, square, triangular, and discoidal form, a fired clay pipe with curved stem and globular bowl, numerous fragments of beaver skins and textile material of twined and twill weaves, part of a large birchbark basket, several pieces of braided rope, some powdered red ocher, and a number of European trade objects. Among these were the remains of two or three brass kettles; about twenty-five iron knife blades, including those of clasp knives and butcher knives; a pair of scissors; iron awls, square in section with an offset crook at the middle; about fifteen iron bracelets; six brass rings; eighteen cylindrical beads probably made of kettle brass; a burning glass; part of the stem of a wineglass; and more than four hundred glass beads. Red beads of round and ring shapes were most common, but the diagnostic polychrome beads included the star or chevron style and beads with inlaid vertical stripes in one or two contrasting colors. Some other beads diagnostic of the Early Historic period were dull red tubular, square, and triangular beads probably made in imitation of native beads of reddish slate and several kinds of stick or bugle beads.

The European trade objects from the ossuary at Ossossane and those from the village site of Cahiague are representative of the Early Historic period. Those from the ossuary at Ossossane cannot be later than 1636 and those from any Huron town or hamlet in Huronia cannot be later than 1650, because by 1651 the Hurons and Petuns had been defeated and driven from their homelands by the Iroquois. In general, then, any Huron or Petun site outside

of the homeland areas should be later than 1650, and it would be
fine if one always could be certain of this. One possible spot that
might manifest a Huron-Petun site of the period between 1650
and 1670 is the Frank Bay site, Lake Nipissing, Ontario (see
Ridley, 1954, pp. 40–50). The uppermost stratum of this important multilevel site contained fragments of Huron-like pottery;
typical styles of Huron pipes and pipe fragments including owl
effigy, vaselike stemless, and acorn varieties; triangular arrowheads of chipped chert or flint; three dog burials; a great many
small pebbles that were polished; and a number of European trade
objects.

The artifacts of European origin consisted of iron and bronze
sword and dagger guards; iron fishhooks and fish spears; bayo-
net fragments; iron awls and knives; three Jesuit rings of brass,
two of which were engraved with a cross and the letters "IHS";
a brass kettle fragment with large rivets on the bracket section;
fragments of kettle brass; bangles or tinklers made of kettle
brass; and some glass beads. According to Ridley (1954, p. 49),
"The European trade material equates with materials found on
mission sites in Huronia, except the beads, which are predomi-
nantly white, and of football shape." It is possible that this particular assemblage of trade goods is representative of a period
between 1650 and 1670. If so, then the top level of the Frank
Bay site may have been the product of refugee Huron and Petun
after their defeat by the Iroquois. It is equally possible that the
top level of the Frank Bay site represents an occupation by the
Algonkian-speaking Nipissing Indians, a proto-Chippewa group.
If this be the case, the Nipissings were either making Huron-like
pottery themselves or obtaining it by trade. Some additional data
and more research might settle the problem of which of these hy-
potheses is correct.

Northern Lake Huron

Westward of the Nipissing there was another proto-Chippewa division of Indians, called Missisauga, who lived along the north
shore of Lake Huron in the Early and Middle Historic periods. A
Frenchman, Antoine Denis Raudot, recorded in 1710 that the Missisauga "live on a river bearing their name, which comes into the
lake [Huron] on the north side. It is abundant with fish, especially

with sturgeon. The members of this tribe all come together in the spring on the bank of this river to plant corn which ripens little. They have from forty-five to sixty warriors and are almost all thieves" (Kinietz, 1940, p. 371). The village site on the bank of the Missisauga River is situated on a sandy plain about a mile upstream from the river mouth. (Fig. 24 illustrates the probable appearance of the village.) In the summer of 1962 excavations at this site were undertaken by the Department of Anthropology of the University of Toronto under the supervision of Dr. Helen Devereux, who kindly allowed me to examine the site and some of the excavated materials. There were European trade goods, triangular arrowheads of chipped flint, an ungrooved axe of ground stone, fragments of Huron-style pipes, and two kinds of pottery. One group of sherds were representative of Huron-like pottery and the other group manifested a variety of a Woodland ware characterized by grit tempering, a cord or fabric impressed surface, flaring rims, and a simple decoration of the rim consisting of cord-wrapped tool impressions vertically placed in one or more encircling rows. This type of pottery should be representative of the Missisauga Indians, and the Huron-like styles ideally should represent trade or Huron potters living among the Missisauga. A pre-

Fig. 24. — Drawing reconstructing a Missisauga Indian village at the end of the Early Historic period. Courtesy of Chicago Natural History Museum.

liminary conclusion was that both types of ceramic wares together with other native cultural materials and the European trade goods were in the same deposits. A consideration of some of the glass beads found in the site suggests the latter part of the Early Historic period and the early portion of the Middle Historic period for the span of the occupancy of this site, but more detailed information will become available after proper study and analysis by archaeologists at the University of Toronto.

The Chequamegon Bay Area

The Chequamegon Bay area on the Lake Superior shore of northernmost Wisconsin should be rich in archaeological remains of the historic period. As early as the autumn of 1659 two French traders, Medard Chouart, Sieur des Groseilliers, and his brother-in-law, Pierre Esprit Radisson, arrived at Chequamegon Bay accompanied by seven canoefuls of Chippewa Indians (Nute, 1959, pp. 3–6, and Ross, 1960, p. 19). In the winter of 1659–60 there was a band of Ottawa Indians in the immediate vicinity and eighteen "nations" of Indians within visiting distance. These "nations" must have been clan or kin groupings that at a later date were subsumed under five or so tribal names. The Huron and Petun who had been driven from their former homelands in the southern Georgian Bay district of Ontario were in the Chequamegon area from 1658 to 1670 (see Kinietz, 1940, p. 2). When Father Claude Jean Allouez arrived in Chequamegon in 1665 there were two large villages in the area, one Huron and the other Ottawa. In 1667 some groups of Potawatomi as well as Sauks and Foxes and Illinois were in the Chequamegon area, probably living among or near the Ottawa. However, in 1670 the Huron moved to Michilimackinac (St. Ignace) and the Ottawa shifted to Manitoulin Island and Michilimackinac (Kinietz, 1940, pp. 3 and 229). Except for small groups that accompanied traders, the Chippewa do not seem to have settled in the Chequamegon area until sometime after 1679 and prior to 1695 (Hickerson, 1962, pp. 66–67, and Kinietz, 1940, p. 319). Thus in the latter part of the Early Historic period the principal tribes of the Chequamegon area were the Ottawa and the Huron, and in the Middle Historic period the dominant Indian occupants of the area were the Chippewa.

Unfortunately the relative abundance of historical data is not matched by the archaeological data. What archaeological evidence is now available from the area has been found on Madeline Island at the mouth of Chequamegon Bay. In the Madeline Island Historical Museum there is a collection of artifacts obtained from locations at the southwestern end of the island. This collection and additional artifacts in the possession of Mr. Al Galazen of La Pointe were examined by me in the summer of 1961 and the autumn of 1963.

The bulk of the pottery was Iroquoian, of styles suggestive of the Huron and Petun, the fragments indicating globular vessels with wide mouths, thickened or collared rims, relatively short necks, and round bottoms. They were made of clay tempered with small particles of rock and fired to tan, gray, or black colors. Vessel surfaces were smooth. Decoration, confined to the collar or thickened rim and the shoulder area, consisted of angular and rectilinear areas of incised lines, sometimes bordered by a row of punctate impressions. Some vessel rims were embellished by the addition of castellations, or decorated loop handles, or both. There were a few sherds indicative of non-Iroquoian pottery. The minority types included a shell-tempered smooth ware with loop handles and incised decoration of Upper Mississippi cultural style, which most likely was Winnebago, and a plain, grit-tempered cord-impressed ware which probably was the product of some Algonkian-speaking group of Indians.

Elbow pipes of fired clay were of typical Huron styles and included acorn, trumpet, barrel, castellated, and effigy forms. Effigies noted on whole pipes or fragments were human heads, a bear head, and what is most likely the head of a pig with carefully delineated snout. Pigs had been introduced into Huronia by the French sometime between 1630 and 1650, and it is most intriguing to note use of the domestic pig as an art motif by a Chequamegon Huron.

Other cultural objects associated with the pottery and pipes were triangular arrowheads of chipped flint, iron arrowheads, French clasp-knife blades of iron, fragments of brass kettles, and long tubular beads of brick-red or blue glass.

Similar artifacts and trade objects have been recovered from the Cadotte site near Grant's Point on southwestern Madeline Island. Excavations made there in the summer of 1961 by Professor Leland R. Cooper of Hamline University revealed the buried remains of a long rectangular house, fragments of pottery, flint arrowheads and other artifacts of native manufacture, as well as European trade goods. Professor Cooper, who is preparing a report on his findings at the Cadotte site, kindly allowed me to examine his collections at Hamline University in April 1963. It seems most probable that some of the materials excavated by Professor Cooper, as well as the previously described collections from Madeline Island, can be attributed primarily to the Huron and Petun. And since the documentary evidence indicates that these Indians were not in the Chequamegon area until after 1650 and and that they left the area in 1670, their cultural remains must date between 1650 and 1670, the latter part of the Early Historic period.

Summary

In the western Great Lakes the Huron and the Petun were the most important groups of Indians during the Early Historic period. In less than sixty years their culture rose from an advanced Stone Age plateau to an Iron Age apogee and then declined to near extinction, against a background of acculturation and warfare engendered by the European fur trade. The events of the Early Historic period were mostly centered in the eastern part of the western Great Lakes region. In the Middle Historic period the central and western parts of the upper Great Lakes region became the centers of interest, and other Indian tribes became the focal point of the fur trade and acculturation.

References

Emerson, 1961; Hickerson, 1962; Kidd, 1953; Kinietz, 1940; Nute, 1959; Popham, 1950; Quimby, 1961–63; Ridley, 1952, 1954; Ross, 1960.

CHAPTER 9

THE ARCHAEOLOGY OF THE MIDDLE
HISTORIC PERIOD, 1670–1760

When La Salle's small trading vessel, the *Griffin*, sailed into the upper Great Lakes region in 1679, she sailed into the Indian world of the Middle Historic period. If there had been a competent anthropologist aboard we would know much more about the Indians of this time and place than we do. Unfortunately the contemporary French observers of this period did not provide the kinds of details that are needed for ethnological and historical reconstruction. One must turn to archaeology for the necessary information.

At the present time in the upper Great Lakes region there are very few known archaeological sites that belong to the Middle Historic period; therefore each of them is a precious document for the study of Indian culture history. Why more such sites are not known to archaeologists is somewhat of a puzzle. Perhaps there were not many to begin with. On the other hand it seems certain that some sites of this period have been destroyed by erosion and the building activities of modern man; several that I know of are now under water. But most probably some additional sites of this period do exist and are merely awaiting discovery. Of the very few known village or cemetery sites of the Middle Historic period, the Bell site is the most completely reported (see Wittry, 1963, pp. 1–57).

Located on the south side of Big Lake Butte des Morts in Winnebago County, Wisconsin, this site was a palisaded village of the Fox Indians from about 1680 to sometime prior to 1730. It seems almost certain that this was the Fox village attacked in 1716 by Louis de la Porte, Sieur de Louvigny, and his army of French and Indians. For instance, Louvigny's artillery consisted of two small brass cannon and a brass grenade mortar. Grenade fragments found at the Bell site were most probably fired from Louvigny's brass mortar during the three days and nights of bombardment suffered by the fortified Fox village, because this engagement was the only one during this period in this section of Wisconsin in which a mortar was fired.

This Fox village was situated on top of a high bank overlooking 300 yards of lower land between it and the waters of Big Lake Butte des Morts. The village was surrounded, according to French observers, by three rows of oak palisades with a ditch in the rear. A portion of the palisade and the ditch were found in the excavations reported by Dr. Wittry. In the middle of the village there was a spring that even in 1959 still produced a supply of fresh water. The dwellings were of at least two kinds, according to the archaeological evidence. One was a bark-covered wigwam manifested in one instance by post holes in a circle 12 feet in diameter and fragments of charred cattail matting and birch bark. The other dwelling style was a rectangular cabin made of poles set into a wall trench and covered probably by mats or sheets of bark (Fig. 25). One such cabin was 30 feet long and 16 feet wide. There were numerous storage and refuse pits that were round or oval in outline and basinlike or bell-shaped in cross section. Some of the shallower of the basinlike pits were used as fireplaces.

The archaeological evidence found at the Bell site indicates that the Fox Indians who inhabited this village were farmers, hunters, fishermen, and gatherers of wild vegetal foods. They raised corn of an eight-row variety and pumpkins or squash (*Cucurbita pepo*). They collected wild plums and probably many other fruits and nuts. They hunted deer, beaver, bear, elk, bison, muskrat, passenger pigeons, ducks, geese, and many other birds and mammals. Fish taken included sturgeon, suckers, buffalo fish, drum, bowfin, catfish, sunfishes, bass, pike, and gar.

Bows and arrows and flintlock guns were used for hunting as well as for warfare. Arrows were tipped with points of chipped flint. Most of the stone arrowheads found at the site were triangular in outline and somewhat crudely chipped (Fig. 26, L, M). They ranged in length from ¾ to 1⅜ inches. There were also arrowheads of conical form made of antler (Fig. 26, I) and a type of beveled bone arrowhead with a bifurcated base (Fig. 26, H). Some arrowheads were made of brass, probably obtained from broken kettles. The common form was conical with a rivet hole for attachment to the shaft, but a thin triangular form was also present. One complete flintlock gun and a number of gun parts were found at the site. European gunflints were tan or honey-colored French spall varieties with round heels. Indian-made gun-

Fig. 25. — Drawing of a hypothetical Indian village in the Green Bay area, *ca.* 1715. Courtesy of Chicago Natural History Museum.

flints were of local chert chipped on both surfaces to a squared outline.

The fishing activities of the Fox Indians were manifested at the Bell site by a single fish lure made of shell (Fig. 26, B) and four bone harpoons of the familiar unilaterally barbed type (Fig. 26, J). Agricultural pursuits were similarly manifested by a fragmentary iron hoe and a hoe made of deer antler.

Various tools found at the Bell site consisted of bone awls, imported iron awls, a small drill of chipped flint, antler drifts or punches, flaking implements of antler, hammerstones, a stone arrowshaft-smoother of the type used in pairs, arrowshaft wrenches

Fig. 26. — Artifacts from the Bell site, a Fox Indian village of the Middle Historic period, 1670–1760. After Wittry (1963). A, ornamented bone arrowshaft straightener; B, fish effigy of shell; C, bone gaming disk; D, engraved bracelet of bone; E, F, decorated bone tubes; G, K, tobacco pipes of fired clay and stone; H, I, arrowheads of bone; J, bone harpoon heads; L, M, arrowheads of chipped flint; N–U, fragments of pottery.

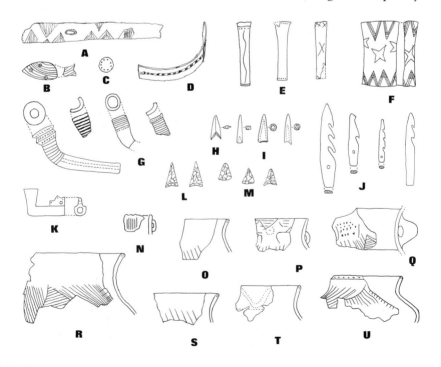

of bone (Fig. 26, A), matting needles made of deer ribs, bone handles for iron awls and knives, an elongated oval knife of chipped flint, French clasp-knife blades of iron (see Fig. 11), sharpening stones, iron trade axes, an iron strike-a-light, butcher knives of iron, a "thumbnail type" scraper of chipped flint, mussel shells used as scrapers, bone fiber-shredders, a long knobbed pin of bone, a bone needle, and a bone paint brush.

Containers of various kinds used by the Fox Indians at the Bell site consisted of bowls made from carapaces of the painted turtle and of Blanding's turtle, brass kettles with lugs, the upper corners of which had been bent over and hammered flat (see Fig. 11), glass bottles, and vessels of native pottery. The dominant pottery type, and thus the one characteristic of Fox Indians, consisted of wide-mouth jars ranging in height from about 6 to 11 inches and from 5 to 10 inches in mouth diameter. The body of such a vessel was spherical with round bottom and a high rim that was nearly straight and outslanting or slightly flaring. Lips were flat with slightly rounded edges and often sloped toward the outside of the jar. Some vessels had strap handles. The clay from which these vessels were made was tempered with crushed gravel and sand and fired to colors ranging from tan to brown. Vessel surfaces were smooth. Decoration, confined to the lip and rim area, was limited to punctating and narrow-line incising. The incised decoration applied to the rim or the junction of rim and shoulder consisted of triangular areas of opposed diagonal lines. Rather closely spaced punctate impressions applied to the vessel lip with a pointed instrument having a trianguloid cross section are characteristic of the Fox Indian pottery at the Bell site (see Fig. 26, N, O, P, Q, R, S, T, U).

Another pottery type present at the site in much smaller quantities was a small globular jar with cord-marked body and a smooth rim that was slightly flaring. The only decoration was a "pie crust" crimping of the outer and inner edges of the lip that produced a kind of scalloped effect. This pottery type is the same as or very similar to that from the prehistoric Dumaw Creek site *circa* 1600 in western Michigan (see Chap. 3). It was made by Potawatomi probably, or possibly Sauk Indians. Other minority styles found at the Bell site include a shell-tempered ware attributable to the Winnebago Indians and grit-tempered styles of the kind made by historic Indians of north central Illinois.

Ornaments found at the Bell site consisted of bracelets made of flat curved bones with lashing holes at the ends and grooves down the outer midline (Fig. 26, D), a bracelet made of brass wire, beads of rolled sheet brass obtained from broken kettles, mirrors, several shapes of pendants made of catlinite, small bone tubes used as beads and hair pipes, large polished bone tubes made from the humerus of the trumpeter swan and decorated with punctates or incised lines (Fig. 26, E, F), and European glass beads. These beads and other trade goods from the Bell site were examined by me in the spring of 1961 with the kind permission and cooperation of Dr. Warren L. Wittry. The glass beads were all representative of the Middle Historic period, 1670–1760. They included the following types: large round or oval (wire-wound or spun) beads of translucent milk glass, round and elongate spheroidal beads of white opaque glass, stick or bugle beads of dark blue color, large runtee or disk-shaped beads of amber color, fluted beads of translucent blue glass, large beads with eight facets (softly rounded where they intersect) in blue, amber, green, or white glass, a large elongate spheroidal bead of opaque white with three groups of blue spiral stripes along the long axis, an elongate spheroidal bead of blue with vertical white stripes in which are centered red stripes, a similar bead of white with blue and red stripes, stick or bugle beads in white with vertical red stripes, and ovoid and "doughnut" shapes in translucent blue or green glass.

Musical or noise-making instruments found at the Bell site consisted of brass hawk bells, conical tinkling cones made of rolled-up trapezoidal sections of thin brass, brass thimbles converted to tinklers, and a jew's-harp of iron. Games indicated by archaeological evidence were dice and bowl, manifested by a bone disk with nine small pits on one side (Fig. 26, C), and the cup and pin game in which were used deer phalanges modified by cutting, grinding, and perforating.

Religious or ceremonial activity reflected in the archaeological evidence included skulls of otter and fisher, so cut as to indicate that they were the remains of medicine bags; remains of fans made from the wings of the great horned owl and the Canada goose; Jesuit rings of brass, possibly given to Christian converts by missionaries; bear ceremonialism manifested by a pit containing a perforated bear skull so placed as to indicate a special treatment and regard; and dog sacrifice represented by a shallow pit containing the articulated skeletons of three dogs.

Tobacco pipes found at the Bell site were of both native and European manufacture. Fragments of white kaolin pipe stems were of European origin. Most of the clay pipes of native manufacture were of Iroquoian style, probably refugee Huron (Fig. 26, G). These were trumpet-form barrel pipes decorated with incising and rows of punctates encircling the bowl. Stem holes were made by modeling the clay around a thick cord of twisted vegetal fiber that burned out during the firing of the clay pipe. Catlinite pipes of typical calumet form were also found (Fig. 26, K). Probably the clay pipes of Iroquoian style and perhaps the catlinite pipes as well were actually made locally by the Fox Indians, although the latter could have been obtained in trade from the Dakota.

The method of burial at the Bell site was inhumation in a flexed or somewhat flexed position with a meager accompaniment of grave goods. In one instance, in what may have been a compound interment, there were the skeletons of a horse and of a male and a female Indian, the male being in a sitting or flexed, upright position.

The social organization of the Fox Indians was similar to that of the Sauk, Miami, Illinois, and Winnebago. They lived in villages, were agricultural, had organized winter hunts in the prairies or park lands, and belonged to various patrilineal clans. Some Fox clan names were Bear, Wolf, Fox, Elk, Swan, Partridge, and Bass. A Fox Indian was a member of the clan of his or her father and could not marry within that clan. The Fox system of reckoning relatives was of the Omaha type and was perplexing to the French because it tended to stress the lineage of one's mother's brother without any regard for separation of generations. For instance, mother's brother was an "uncle" and his male descendants through males were "uncles" regardless of their age or generation. The daughters of these uncles were called mother; thus any reasonable Frenchman might have thought mistakenly that a Fox Indian was lying when he claimed that a female child was an old man's mother. Be that as it may, the kind of social organization possessed by the Fox was indicative of a milder and richer environment and of greater wealth and a more sedentary life than was enjoyed by more northerly peoples such as the Ottawa and Chippewa.

The clothing of the Fox Indians was variable. The men wore only a breechcloth and moccasins in warm weather; but for winter they had deerskin or elkskin shirts and leggings, topped by robes of beaver or buffalo skins. These robes were sometimes embroidered with flattened, dyed porcupine quills or decorated with painted designs. Winter clothing for women included dresses of elkskin or deerskin, leggings, and moccasins, while in summer they probably wore only a skirt and moccasins. At the time of the occupation of the Bell site by Fox Indians, cloth received in trade from the French would have been used to a considerable degree in the manufacture of their clothing, and even French garments probably were in use along with the older styles of skin clothing.

The division of labor between men and women was generally as follows: The women worked in the fields, did the planting and harvesting, gathered wild vegetal foods, made clothing and pottery, collected firewood and did the cooking, took care of children, wove mats, baskets, and bags, and engaged in household activities. The men cleared land for the fields, made tools, weapons, and some utensils, engaged in hunting and warfare, made wooden dugout canoes, and were the major participants in political and religious activities.

The Fox Indians who occupied the Bell site in the early years of the eighteenth century were already somewhat acculturated by fifty years or more of contact with French traders and missionaries. Yet this was an interesting and archaeologically significant point on the regional scale of culture change brought about by contact with Europeans. For one thing, flintlock guns, although in use by the Indians, had not yet completely replaced the bow and flint-tipped arrow. The use of imported brass kettles had not yet supplanted the manufacture and use of native pottery. Although the technological aspects of Fox culture had been changed considerably, the material links with the prehistoric culture of the Fox Indians had not been lost. Knowledge of a site such as this one enables us to link the prehistoric period with the Fox Indian culture of the Late Historic period, by which time Fox culture had merged with the Pan-Indian fur trade culture to a point where all native manufactures of primary archaeological interest had been superseded by imported artifacts.

Another Indian site of the Middle Historic period is the Gros Cap cemetery, 5 miles west of St. Ignace in Mackinac County, Michigan. This site is somewhat of a contrast to the Bell site in that it is essentially a cemetery. It also probably occupies a place slightly later in the Middle Historic period than the Bell site, or else it lasted longer within the period.

The Indians who made use of the Gros Cap cemetery site in the Middle Historic period often buried their dead in an extended position on their backs with hands on the chest. Some sort of cremation was also practiced. One such instance is illustrated by the recovery of a small chest or ornamented box containing burned human bones. This chest, in a fragmentary condition when found, originally must have been impressively ornate. Measuring about 24 inches long, 15 inches wide, and 10 inches high, it was made of wood covered with leather, bound with brass straps, and fitted with an iron handle, lock, and key. The leather covering of the box was studded with brass nails that had ornamental heads and were arranged in a curvilinear pattern which in part consisted of groups of adjoining circles joined by curved lines. Fragments of a similar chest were found at the Bell site. Also found at the Bell site was an iron key very similar to the key associated with this chest from the Gros Cap cemetery site. Those Indians who were buried in the flesh (not cremated) were accompanied by various kinds of artifacts of native and European manufacture. With one burial, for instance, there were the following objects: one stylized animal effigy of bone, 3½ inches long (Fig. 27, B); nineteen hawk bells of brass, four of which were attached to a fragmentary string of ten spheroidal beads of blue glass; nine egg-shaped (wire-wound type) beads of milk glass; fourteen blue glass beads with eight facets, slightly rounded at the intersections of the planes or facets; four tubular beads of blue glass ¾ to 1½ inches long; thirty elongate spheroidal beads of white opaque glass; three similar beads but marked with spiral stripes in blue and brown; two elongate spheroidal polychrome beads of white opaque glass with two opposing bands of three closely spaced spiral stripes of blue; one square pendant made of marine shell; and one small fine-toothed comb (of tortoise shell) that would have been ideal for head lice. The comb, the hawk bells, and the glass beads were trade objects of European manufacture. The shell pendant and the animal effigy of carved bone were artifacts of native manufacture. The types of glass beads indicate that the burial dates from 1700 or later; and the lack of any silver ornaments suggests that this particular burial is earlier than 1760.

Another burial, the skeleton of an adult Indian, was accompanied by two bone needles for weaving mats, four brass hawk bells that likely were attached to clothing, and ten Jesuit finger rings of brass. The ten rings were all associated with one hand and

Fig. 27. — Artifacts of bone and stone from the Gros Cap site, Middle Historic period, 1670–1760. Courtesy of Chicago Natural History Museum. A, human effigy; B, bone animal effigy; C, bone spoon; D, artifact from pig tusk; E, F, G, M, Q, bone harpoon heads; H, bone tool; I, P, bone needles; J, bone wristband; K, L, bone arrowheads; N, O, flint arrowheads.

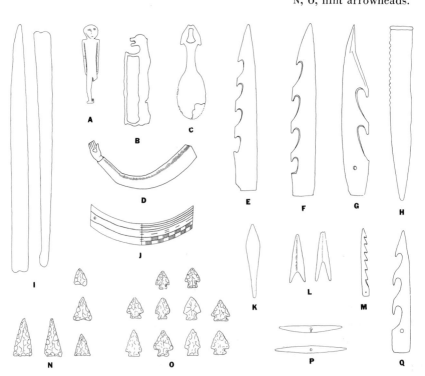

apparently were worn as a group; but on which hand, or how many per finger unfortunately is not recorded. Presumably this particular burial was that of a Christian convert. And although brass Jesuit rings have been found at other historic period sites, this is the only instance, in my experience, where a number of rings were found on one hand. The presence of these rings in this specific context suggests a date sometime between 1670 and 1760.

A burial of an Indian mother and child in one grave was associated with the following native artifacts and trade objects: a bone wristband with an engraved rectilinear design consisting of parallel lines and hachured rectangles (Fig. 27, J), a pointed bone tool 6½ inches long (Fig. 27, H), four opaque white glass beads of elongated spheroidal form, six round beads of opaque white glass, one round bead of blue glass, two round beads of dull red glass, and five very small (seed) beads of blue glass. A C-shaped bracelet of thick brass wire was found in association with the skeletal remains of the child.

Still another burial, presumably an adult, had associated with it the following artifacts, listing first those of native manufacture: one small effigy of an eagle made of marine shell, two large tubular beads, also of marine shell, one rectanguloid pendant made of marine shell and perforated for suspension, one bone harpoon head (Fig. 27, M) 3 inches long with six barbs on one side and a wedgelike base with a line hole in it, and a larger harpoon head of bone (Fig. 27, Q) 4¾ inches long, with three barbs all on one side, and a wedge-shaped base with a line hole. There were also some sixty brass tinkling cones about ¾ inch long and twelve larger cones about 1½ inches in length. Many of these tinkling cones of both sizes were filled with tufts of human hair at the open end and had twisted cord or leather fragments at their apexes indicating that they once had been attached to something. There were also three small round (seed) beads of blue glass, a fragment of European cloth stained green by metal salts, and a triangular arrowhead of brass with slitlike side notches. A fragment of human skin with hair attached may have been a scalp but also may have been an ordinary part of the original burial particularly well preserved by metal salts.

Elsewhere in the Gros Cap cemetery site there was unearthed a skull with the ear openings plugged with molten lead. Many other burials have been found in this site, but unfortunately specific data about the position of the skeletons and their grave associations are lacking. There are, however, data on a number of trade objects and artifacts that were found with such burials and which collectively may be considered a sample of the burial furniture from the Gros Cap cemetery site. The materials which I have examined are as follows.

Native artifacts made of bone consisted of two flat mat needles 7 and 8 inches long (Fig. 27, I), a spoon 4 inches long with an ornamental handle (Fig. 27, C), a human effigy about 4 inches long (Fig. 27, A), a polished tube 4 inches long, a fragmentary pin or peg about 3½ inches long with knobbed head, an awl made from a deer metapodial, a flat, narrow fragment of bone with a cross-hatched design engraved on it, a tabular pendant with a hole drilled into it, a large antler chipping tool, five small antler awls or chipping tools, two unilaterally barbed harpoon heads, each 6½ inches long with four barbs and a wedge-shaped base (Fig. 27, E, F), one unilaterally barbed harpoon head with two barbs (probably three barbs originally) with a wedge-shaped base and a line hole drilled with a metal drill (Fig. 27, G), a fragment of a unilaterally barbed harpoon head, two arrowheads with bifurcated bases (Fig. 27, L), one arrowhead with leaf-shaped blade and long narrow tang (Fig. 27, K), three antler drifts, two socketed conical points of antler, two double-pointed bodkins or snowshoe needles 2½ inches long, each with a drilled hole at the mid-point (Fig. 27, P), and a hollow object shaped like a truncated cone with two drilled holes near the base and a knotted piece of leather inserted through the hollow portion. This may have been part of a headdress or perhaps some kind of swivel.

An interesting item of apparel was a fragmentary belt or band of leather about 1 inch wide and 12 inches long, upon which were fastened small tubular beads of brass or copper about ⅛ inch long. The beads were closely spaced and arranged in five parallel rows that produced the illusion of a solid mass of metal beads.

Artifacts presumably of native origin and made of catlinite consisted of a human effigy face or miniature masklike object 1¼ inches long (Fig. 28, E), two beaver effigy pendants, each about 1 inch long, nine beads or pendants of trianguloid or rectanguloid form ranging from ½ to 1 inch in length, three V-shaped beads about ½ inch long, one wheel-shaped bead or pendant ¾ inch in diameter (Fig. 28, K), one square pendant with large round center removed (Fig. 28, L), and a heart-shaped ornament 1¼ inches long with three small holes drilled through it, one at each extremity (Fig. 28, J). A pendant 1½ inches long, shaped like a turtle, on a necklace of eight V-shaped beads in alternate sequence with seven slightly biconoidal or tubular beads (Fig. 28, F) completes the inventory of catlinite objects from the general part of the Gros Cap cemetery site collection.

A unique artifact made from a pig tusk about 4 inches long is a carving of the representation of an arm and right hand with a heart in the palm (Fig. 27, D). The concept expressed is non-

Fig. 28. — Pottery and other artifacts from the Gros Cap site, Middle Historic period, 1670–1760. Courtesy of Chicago Natural History Museum. A, B, I, tobacco pipes of stone; C, H, O, tobacco pipes of clay; D, pottery jar; E, human effigy face, of catlinite; F, J, K, L, catlinite pendants; G, shell runtee; M, N, fish effigies of shell.

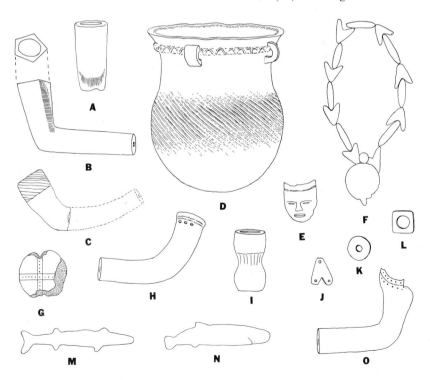

Indian and European. It could be the product of an acculturated Indian, or it could have been acquired by an Indian from a
French *voyageur*. It also raises the possibility that on cultural
grounds alone the archaeologist dealing with the historic period
cannot distinguish between burials of acculturated Indians and
those of *voyageurs* who died in the region.

Native artifacts made of imported marine shell found at the
Gros Cap cemetery site were five tubular beads about 1½ inches
long, a trianguloid pendant about 1¼ inches long, a rectanguloid
section of shell about 1½ inches long, an effigy of a fish 4½
inches long (Fig. 28, M), and another fish effigy (Fig. 28, N)
somewhat smaller. These effigies probably were used as fish lures.

Tobacco pipes of native manufacture seem to represent Iroquoian styles and probably are Huron in origin. It is likely that
the Huron at near-by Michilimackinac made pipes for trade with
their neighbors. It is also possible that other Indians were copying
Huron styles. The pipes from the Gros Cap cemetery site include
an elbow form of fired clay (Fig. 28, O) with a castellated bowl,
the upper part of which is ornamented with a single incised line
and two rows of punctate impressions, a polished stone elbow pipe
4 inches long with a bowl pentagonal in section and the stem hexagonal in section (Fig. 28, B), a trumpet-shaped pipe of fired clay
with a simple line and punctate decoration around the upper part
of the bowl (Fig. 28, H), and a similar but fragmentary pipe with
oblique parallel incised lines in a band around the bowl (Fig.
28, C). There are also two or three large portions of stems from
fired clay pipes of the style last described. Of two other pipes from
the Gros Cap cemetery site one is a modified Micmac form (Fig.
28, I) of soft stone; and the other, also of stone, is vaselike
(Fig. 28, A). These pipes required wooden or reed stems for
their use.

Some aboriginal pottery has been found at the site. In the collection examined by me there were eleven body sherds of a ware
characterized by smooth vessel surfaces and made of a clay mixed
with small particles of shell before firing, as well as nine similar
body sherds made of a clay that had been mixed with small particles of granitic stone before firing. One large rim sherd with a
smooth, undecorated surface was tempered with small particles
of both shell and granitic rock. This sherd manifests a vessel with

a straight rim and a slightly rounded lip that is ornamented with shallow notches somewhat widely spaced. A smaller rim sherd that is grit-tempered has a rounded lip upon which are somewhat closely spaced punctate impressions. There was one slightly flaring rim, grit-tempered with narrowed and rounded lip, that had a notched fillet or narrow collar midway between neck and lip. Two additional grit-tempered rim sherds manifest vessels with smooth exteriors, slightly flaring rims and rounded lips. One of these sherds is ornamented with somewhat closely spaced notches along the outer edge of the lip. A similarly ornamented rim sherd, grit-tempered, and slightly flaring, has a loop handle extending from the lip to the neck area.

There were two whole vessels in the collection I examined. One was a miniature jar about 1½ inches in height. It is a shell-tempered vessel with rounded bottom, short body, slightly flaring rim, and broad orifice. The outer edge of the lip is ornamented with notches somewhat closely spaced. Such a miniature jar may have been a toy or, more likely, a part of the burial furniture placed with a deceased child.

One nearly complete jar about 8 inches high (Fig. 28, D) has a round bottom, a relatively short body, a constriction of the upper shoulder or neck, and a flaring rim. It is made of fired clay tempered with particles of shell and grit. The rim area is smooth, but the body of the jar shows the imprint of a fabric or a cord-wrapped paddle. The lip is rounded, and about ¾ inch beneath it there is a notched fillet encircling the vessel. Four strap handles, equally spaced around the rim, extend from this fillet to the neck of the jar. The vessel mouth is quite broad. This jar is similar to some of the unclassified pottery found at the Bell site and to pottery found at a late seventeenth-century village near Starved Rock in Illinois.

A few arrowheads of chipped flint have been found at the Gros Cap cemetery site. There are about a half dozen small triangular points from ½ to 1 inch in length (Fig. 27, N). Some of these are neatly chipped on both faces, whereas others have minimal chipping that is used to modify the flake only where necessary to produce the desired triangular form. These two variants of tri-angular points are found frequently in protohistoric and Early Historic period sites of the upper Great Lakes region. There were also about a dozen small corner-notched arrowheads of triangu-loid outline (Fig. 27, o). The chipping was similar to that of the triangular forms. The corner-notched points ranged from about ¾ to 1¼ inches.

The trade objects from the Gros Cap cemetery site, which have to be considered collectively because they are lacking specific proveniences within the site, probably were placed with burials originally. This probability is suggested by the few clusters of burial furniture of known association within the site plus experi-ence with similar sites elsewhere. However, there may be some trade objects that were part of the camp debris at the site. An inventory of those trade objects from the site, but without specific locations, is as follows: There was a barbed spear point of iron 4½ inches long with a "rat tail" shank; three French clasp-knife blades of the hawk bill variety about 4¼ inches long; several fragments of such blades; two iron awls; a dozen wrought-iron nails of various sizes; four butcher knives, two of which still have wooden handles; a broken fire steel or strike-a-light; a barbed arrowhead of iron; a fragmentary pewter disk, possibly a por-ringer, about 4½ inches in diameter; some fragments of cloth; and some masses of powdered vermilion.

There was a roughcast button of brass with a hole drilled in the shank (a style in vogue from 1700 to 1765), at least eleven tinkling cones made of sheet brass from broken kettles, four frag-ments of brass kettles including one riveted lug section with upper corners bent over and pounded flat, several brass hawk bells, five brass coils that may have been ear ornaments or broken sections of a spring type hair-puller, and three Jesuit finger rings of brass. There was also an oval religious medal of brass or bronze.

There were several blond gunflints of spall type with round heels, one of which was altered as if it had been used with a strike-a-light for making fire; three runtees of marine shell, one of which was decorated with a cross and dot design (Fig. 28, G); and several fragments of kaolin pipe stems, one of which had "Glasgow" stamped on it. One bulldog effigy pipe of white kaolin was made by "Gambier à Paris," according to the legend stamped upon its base. These pipes, probably out of context here, repre-sent a later period.

The glass beads from the general site collection seem to duplicate most of those found in specific burial associations at the Gros Cap cemetery site. There were nineteen large, spheroidal milk glass beads (of wire-wound type) about ¾ inch in length, thirty similar but smaller beads ⅜ inch long, sixty decahedral beads of blue glass rounded at the intersection of the facets, nineteen elongated spheroidal beads of opaque white glass ⅜ to 1½ inch in length, two round beads of blue glass, a dozen football-shaped beads of green glass ⅜ inch long, a large mulberry-shaped bead of clear glass, a lopsided teardrop bead of clear glass, two spheroidal beads ⅜ inch long of blue glass with vertical white stripes, and an elongated spheroidal bead of blue glass with three inlaid vertical bars of white with a red stripe centered in each white bar.

Some additional beads from the Gros Cap cemetery site were on display in the historical museum at Escanaba, Michigan, where I examined them in the summer of 1963. There was a spheroidal bead of white glass with black spiral lines, five elongated spheroidal beads of opaque white glass, a spheroidal bead (wire-wound type) of milk glass about ½ inch long, nine spheroidal beads of blue glass, two elongated spheroidal beads of blue glass, each inlaid with three white spirals which had red center stripes, a green glass spheroidal bead with spiral stripes of white, and a small white tubular bead with vertical red stripes. Also in this collection from the Gros Gap cemetery site there were nine tinkling cones of brass and a shell runtee.

Faunal remains were not abundant. I was able to identify remains of sturgeon, turtle, deer, bear, beaver, hawk or eagle, canid, and pig. Items such as hawk or eagle claws, bear canines, beaver incisors and beaver jaws, turtle shell, and jaws of dog or wolf probably were charms, parts of medicine bags, or ornaments. Sections of hollow bird bone likely served some utilitarian need. Arrowheads and awls were made of deer bone, and one ornament or religious object was made of a pig tusk. About the only remains that could be considered absolutely indicative of food were those of sturgeon and other large fish.

The cultural picture that emerges from a study of the artifacts and their context is that of a group of somewhat acculturated Indians living at Gros Cap on the shore of Lake Michigan and burying their dead on an old beach terrace some distance back of the shore. Although some or perhaps all of these Indians were converts to Christianity, they had not abandoned the old ways, but had merely altered them in varying degrees.

In lieu of documentary evidence the clue to the age of the Gros Cap cemetery site lies in the use of the trade objects as chronological indicators. This particular assemblage of trade objects is representative of the Middle Historic period; it definitely does not fit the Early Historic period prior to 1670, nor does it fit the Late Historic period that began in 1760. The specific varieties of glass beads suggest a date later than 1700; thus I would conclude that the proper chronological position of the Gros Cap cemetery site is in the latter part of the Middle Historic period, say about 1710 to 1760.

Who were the Indians who lived at Gros Cap between 1710 and 1760? Without historical records what clues to their identity are available? For one thing the native pipes from the site are of Huron styles, yet the aboriginal pottery is non-Huron. This pottery, limited as it is, suggested tribal relations in the direction of Sauk, Fox, Miami, and Illinois. The arrowheads of chipped flint suggest these tribes but also Potawatomi, Chippewa, Ottawa, and Huron. Historical evidence indicates that Ottawa and Huron were the principal native residents of near-by Michilimackinac at about 1700 but there were also representatives of all of the above-named tribes in the area from time to time. I would guess that the Indians who lived at Gros Cap in the first half of the eighteenth century were mainly Ottawa and that there was a smattering of female slaves or wives from such tribes as the Illinois, Miami, Sauk, Fox, and Potawatomi. Since there were Huron pipes but no Huron pottery, I do not believe that there were Huron women in this community. The Huron pipe styles were either copied by the Ottawa or else the pipes were obtained from French traders or directly from the Huron. And lastly, the Gros Cap Indians, whoever they were, had many traits in common with the Fox Indians at the Bell site in Wisconsin.

In August 1679 when La Salle's sailing vessel, the *Griffin*, visited Michilimackinac there were two villages of Indians who had settled there within the past ten years. One of these villages was Huron, the other was Ottawa. Some 279 years later, in April 1958, a cemetery belonging to one or the other of these two villages was accidentally discovered by excavators who were digging

for gravel with a power shovel (see Greenman, 1958, pp. 28–35).
The site of this cemetery was a bluff about 80 feet above Lake
Huron at the northeastern edge of St. Ignace, Michigan. Here in
what appears to have been a mass burial place or ossuary were
found the remains of fifty-two individuals, most of whom were
adults.

With the skeletons there were a number of artifacts, the majority being trade goods obtained from European sources. There
were two brass kettles, twenty-two brass tinkling cones, three hawk
bells of brass, a runtee of marine shell, glass beads of several
kinds, and three brass coils or ear screws $\frac{5}{8}$ inch in diameter.
Ear screws of the Ottawa Indians were described by Pierre Esprit
Radisson (see Kinietz, 1940, p. 235) as follows: "Their ears have
ordinarily 5 holes, where one may putt the end of his finger.
They use those holes in this sort: to make themselves gallant they
pass through it a skrew of coper [sic]. . . . They fill those skrews
with swan's downe. . . ." The shell runtee, a disk-shaped pendant
with two parallel holes drilled edgeways through the middle, was
decorated with four quadrant ellipses whose apexes met at the
center. Undoubtedly this decoration was incised with a steel compass. The glass beads consisted of the following: sixty-five spheroidal beads of opaque black ranging from $\frac{3}{16}$ to $\frac{1}{4}$ inch in diameter, a dark blue spheroidal bead about $\frac{3}{8}$ inch in diameter, two
spheroidal beads of opaque white about $\frac{1}{4}$ inch in diameter, a
slightly elongated spheroidal bead of opaque white about $\frac{3}{8}$ inch
long and with a small nib or drawn-out projection at the hole,
thirty-one small white opaque seed beads, and a similar seed bead
of light blue opaque glass.

Artifacts of native manufacture found in the ossuary were two
lumps of red ochre, an effigy of a human face $1\frac{1}{4}$ inches high and
made of carved antler, a leather thong upon which were strung
nine beads of copper or possibly of brass from discarded kettles,
and a broken pipe of cream-colored polished stone about 4 inches
long. The upper bowl portion of this pipe is carved in the form
of a hawk or an eagle. A part of the stem is missing, probably
half. This is a Huron style of tobacco pipe.

Within 15 feet of the ossuary further excavation revealed a
shallow pit in which were the skeletons of two dogs — archaeological evidence of the sacrifice of dogs, which was a common

custom of the Indians of the region throughout the historic period.

The trade goods associated with the ossuary, although somewhat meager, do indicate a dating within the Middle Historic period. The glass beads seem so limited in styles present that I suspect some unknown and unusual factor of selection. It is as if all polychrome or brightly colored monochrome beads were taboo or had been removed from this assemblage. Yet the larger beads, insofar as they are represented in the collection from the ossuary are representative of the Middle Historic period.

The ossuary itself is a place of burial associated with the Feast of the Dead, a rite practiced by both the Huron (see Chap. 8) and the Ottawa. The last recorded date for a performance of the Feast of the Dead at Michilimackinac was 1682, and it was undertaken by the Ottawa (Greenman, 1958, p. 31). The ossuary just described could have been the mass burial associated with that particular ceremony. However, there may have been other, unrecorded, mass burials in the vicinity of St. Ignace, Michigan, during the Middle Historic period, and the few artifacts found with the skeletons in the St. Ignace ossuary are just as indicative of the refugee Huron as of the local Ottawas.

In Mackinaw City, Michigan, just across the straits from St. Ignace, there is the historic site of Fort Michilimackinac. Archaeological excavations there have produced aboriginal cultural remains some of which are in a context dated at about 1715 to 1760 (see Maxwell, 1964). These cultural remains include the following: twenty-one small triangular arrowheads of chipped flint, two similar arrowheads chipped from green bottle glass, one small corner-notched arrowhead of chipped flint, a bone arrowhead with bifurcated base, a bone arrowhead with a flat base, a conical arrowhead made of antler, four large harpoon heads made of elk antler with barbs on one side and a line hole at the base, six antler handles for iron awls, two snowshoe needles made of antler, a bone awl, two large hide-dressers of bone, a scraper made of deer or elk leg bone, and some tubes of polished bird bone. Decorative objects consist of a bone awl handle ornamented with two bands of circular indentations, two disklike buttons of antler, a flat bone pendant carved to represent an animal head, a fox canine tooth perforated for use as a bead or pendant, and a small gaming disk of bone with a row of drilled dots around the periphery.

These artifacts and native pottery to be described presently were in general association with a tremendous quantity of trade objects representative of the Middle Historic period. This of course is not unexpected, because Fort Michilimackinac in its period was the center of the fur trade in the western Great Lakes. The trade objects — glass beads, iron knives, kettles, metal arrowheads, shell beads, bottles, brass rings, awls, stone and kaolin pipes, etc. — are all similar to those from the Gros Cap cemetery site and other sites of the Middle Historic period in the western Great Lakes region, but appear in far greater abundance at Fort Michilimackinac than they do elsewhere.

The pottery of native manufacture was manifested by about 750 grit-tempered sherds of four or five general styles. In the first category of style were fragments representing a round bottomed jar with a slightly constricted neck and a slightly flaring rim with squared lip. External surfaces were covered with cord impressions probably from a cord-wrapped paddle. A variant of this style, observed by me on visits to the Fort Michilimackinac excavations, had finger notching along the lip, and seems to be similar to pottery from the Dumaw Creek site in western Michigan and to one of the minor types from the Bell site in northeastern Wisconsin. The second style is, according to Dr. Moreau Maxwell (1964, p. 26):

what has long been called Lake Michigan ware, a grit-tempered, cord-roughened ware which covers a long time span and many stylistic variants. Sherds of this type at Fort Michilimackinac have thin, broad filets applied to the rim, or rounded, thick filets rolled over the top of the rim. The rim area, often on interior as well as exterior, is decorated with varying impressions made by cord-wrapped paddle edges or with the sharp corner of an unwrapped paddle. Lips of these vessels were usually notched with paddle edges.

The vessel shapes are similar to that of the first category previously described.

The third pottery type, represented by only three sherds, was similar to a type found among the Winnebago of Wisconsin and the bearers of the Blue Island culture in northeastern Illinois. The fourth style, actually the most common in the counts of rim sherds, consisted of round bottomed jars with constricted necks, slightly flaring rims, and orifices smaller than the shoulder diameter. According to Maxwell (1964, p. 27) this ware

is grit tempered, smooth surfaced, usually with firing cracks on the surface, and decorated on the rim and lip with sharply incised lines, usually in chevrons. The lip is pulled out and down, usually diagonally, to form the rim. This treatment is distinct from the [rim] filleting of the second pottery style. On at least two rim sherds from different vessels there are small strap handles.

Dr. Maxwell suggests that this style of pottery was characteristic of the local Indian population, most of whom were Ottawa. His suggestion would gain considerable support if similar pottery were to be found in the St. Ignace and Chequamegon Bay areas and other known places of Ottawa occupancy in the early part of the Middle Historic period.

About 250 miles north of the Straits of Mackinac, where the Pic River enters the north side of Lake Superior, there is a stratified site of considerable interest (see Quimby, 1961, pp. 83–89, and Wright, 1963, pp. 5–6). The top stratum of the Pic River site contained aboriginal cultural remains and European trade objects representative of the Middle Historic period. Two lower strata lacked any evidence of European contact, and the lowermost stratum of the two has produced organic remains radiocarbon-dated at A.D. 950 plus or minus 80 years. What is here important about the Pic River site is that the Late Woodland culture manifested there persists into the Middle Historic period and thus represents a very early, or even first, contact between Europeans and the particular proto-Chippewa group or groups who were native to the area in this period. The top stratum of the Pic River site contained not only trade objects representative of the Middle Historic period but also aboriginal pottery, arrowheads, and other weapons, tools, utensils, and ornaments. According to J. V. Wright (1963, p. 6),

this stratum almost certainly represents an Ojibway [Chippewa] occupation. . . . The pottery from this historic stratum represents a mixture of at least two ceramic traditions. A modified form of the Black-duck/Manitoba foci is still present. Markedly different [vessels] are represented by collared rims with horizontal rows of push-pull [incising.] Another common feature of these rims is the occurrence of horizontal rows of push-pull on the interior of the rim just below the lip. These sherds strongly resemble specimens from the Upper Michigan peninsula. From another portion of the site, where very little aboriginal material occurred with historic refuse, a shell and grit-tempered Upper Mississippi body sherd and a grit-tempered fabric-impressed rim sherd were recovered.

The range of ceramic styles in the top stratum of the Pic River site is similar to that of late prehistoric Woodland sites in the Straits of Mackinac and along the shores of northern Lake Michigan as far west as Seul Choix Point and along the shores of Whitefish Bay in Lake Superior. Probably all of these sites represent ancestral Chippewa groups, and in the case of the Pic River site we have good evidence that a proto-Chippewa group is responsible for the majority of the aboriginal remains found in the top stratum. Historic sites along the east shore of Lake Superior at the mouth of the Michipicotin and Montreal rivers contained Huron and Petun ceramics in association with trade objects of the Middle Historic period and may represent occupancies by the refugee Huron, by the Missisauga, or by a combination of both.

SUMMARY

Of the few known sites from the Middle Historic period, the Bell site, in Winnebago County, Wisconsin, has been most completely recorded. This was a palisaded village of Fox Indians which represented an interesting transitional stage in the acculturation process, manifesting numerous material links with prehistoric culture yet increasingly affected by contact with Europeans. Another important site of the Middle Historic period was essentially a burial place rather than a village. This was the Gros Cap cemetery site in Mackinac County, Michigan, where the association of native artifacts and European trade objects indicated a somewhat greater degree of acculturation than at the Bell site. The Gros Cap Indians were, by my guess, mainly Ottawa.

Other significant sites from the middle period were an ossuary near St. Ignace, Michigan; the historic site of Fort Michilimackinac, the center of the fur trade; and the Pic River site, which manifests a Late Woodland proto-Chippewa culture in association with trade objects of the Middle Historic period.

REFERENCES

Greenman, 1958; Kinietz, 1940; Maxwell, 1964; Quimby, 1961 and field notes; Wittry, 1963; Wright, 1963.

CHAPTER 10

THE ARCHAEOLOGY OF THE LATE
HISTORIC PERIOD, 1760–1820

With some rare exceptions the archaeology of the Late Historic period has not been studied by professional archaeologists, most of whom choose to work with more ancient cultures and periods. Nevertheless there are some interesting assemblages of archaeological data from sites excavated accidentally by construction workers, farmers, and the like, or from sites explored by amateur archaeologists. These data can be usefully employed in the cultural descriptions and analyses of the Late Historic period. For instance, they clearly show that by 1760 or shortly afterwards the Indians of the western Great Lakes region had discarded most of their material culture in favor of new things introduced by fur traders. This was one of the major factors that led to the creation of a Pan-Indian culture in the region.

In terms of the kinds of classifications used by archaeologists when dealing with prehistoric cultures, the cultures of the Late Historic period seem to belong in one category. This was not true of the cultures of the Middle and Early Historic periods, even though the same kinds of acculturational forces were operative then. The tribal cultures were still intact and differentiated. In the Late Historic period the tribal cultures were submerged and subsumed by the Pan-Indian culture of the region. This culture was manifested by various bands and tribes of Indians who made their living by hunting and trapping for European and American commercial interests. Their principal product was beaver fur, which they exchanged for liquor, tools, weapons, utensils, ornaments, food, medicine, and any other thing supplied by traders. In the following pages I have presented samples of this Late Historic period Pan-Indian culture arranged in terms of tribes and territories.

THE SAUK AND FOX

The Sauk and Fox were separate but closely related tribes at the beginning of the Middle Historic period when they lived in the Green Bay area. By the beginning of the Late Historic period these two tribes had united in a loose confederacy and had moved southward and westward. In 1959–1961 a Sauk village and cemetery site in Illinois, along the Rock River near its junction with the Mississippi, was excavated by the University of Illinois under the direction of Dr. Elaine Bluhm. Preliminary reports indicated that the site was occupied at a time (about 1790–1810) after the Sauk had left the upper Great Lakes region and that the village consisted of houses arranged in a row along a low ridge parallel to the river (*American Antiquity Notes and News*, 1960, p. 630; 1961, p. 586). At least eight houses were found by the excavators. The houses were large rectangular structures with supporting walls of vertical poles and were probably covered with elm bark. There were numerous fire pits, storage pits, and refuse pits. Some of the fire pits contained charred corn.

Among the excavated artifacts indicative of trade with white men were parts and accessories of flintlock guns, iron knives, brass kettle fragments, iron axes, silver ornaments made in Canada and the United States, kaolin pipes, and glass beads.

These Indians had learned the white man's technique of smelting lead from ores and were casting bullets and other objects of this metal at the time of occupancy of the site. Some stone pipes and various articles made of bone, such as knife handles, weaving implements, and hair ornaments seem to have been old-style native manufactures and may reflect a conservatism in some aspects of material culture. Such manufactures go back to the Middle and Early Historic periods when the Sauk were residing in the upper Great Lakes region before they drifted into the upper Mississippi Valley. The complete report on this site should supply the first description and analysis of a scientifically controlled excavation of a Late Historic period village in the upper Great Lakes or adjacent regions.

Peter Pond, a fur trader who was a firsthand observer of the Sauk between 1773 and 1775 recorded the following account (see Hewitt, 1912, p. 476; I have regularized the spelling and punctuation):

These people are called Sauk. They are of good size and well disposed — less inclined to tricks and bad manners than their neighbors. . . . Some of their huts are sixty feet long and contain several families [each]. . . . In the fall of the year they leave their huts and go into the woods in quest of game and return in the spring to their huts before planting time. The women raise large crops of corn, beans, pumpkins, [and] melons. . . . The land is excellent — and clear of wood for some distance from the village. There are some hundreds of inhabitants. Their amusements are singing, dancing, smoking, contests, gambling games, feasting, drinking, sleight of hand tricks, hunting, and they are famous in magic [shamanism and magico-religious acts]. They are not very jealous of their women. In general the women find means to gratify themselves without the consent of the men. The Sauk warriors often join war parties of neighboring tribes against the Indians who live along the Missouri River and sometimes they go to the vicinity of Sante Fe, New Mexico, to capture Spanish horses of which they had a large number.

THE POTAWATOMI

In the Late Historic period the Potawatomi were the Indians dominant in the areas adjacent to the southern one-third of Lake Michigan. At this time, 1760 to 1820 and even somewhat later, Potawatomi villages were scattered from Milwaukee southward into northern Illinois, eastward into northern Indiana, and across southern Michigan, particularly in the valley of the St. Joseph River (see Tucker, 1942, maps 29, 38, 46, 48, and 49). In most instances the names of these villages are a matter of historical record and even the names of the band or village chiefs are known. Because of this relatively abundant documentation it seems virtually certain that the archaeological remains dating between 1760 and 1820 or so which have been found in the vicinity of a known Potawatomi settlement must be attributable to the Potawatomi. For instance, in the Chicago Natural History Museum there is a collection of materials found in 1928 associated with extended skeletons in shallow graves along the Des Plaines River in Channahon Township, Will County, Illinois. These burials most probably were Potawatomi.

In the graves, as burial furnishings for the deceased, were ornaments, utensils, weapons, and tools. These included a unilaterally barbed point of bone for a fish spear, a brass kettle, a small alcohol lamp of brass, an iron axe, two small glass vials marked "Essence of Peppermint by the Kings Patent" (on one bottle the spelling is "Pepermint"), fragments of cloth, brass thimbles used as tinklers along the fringes of garments, cones of sheet brass used as tinklers, and morris bells or hawk bells of brass that were also attached to clothing so that the wearer produced a soft, rhythmical tinkling sound as he or she moved.

Silver ornaments found with the dead included at least eight pairs of earbobs, five miniature round brooches, five miniature double-barred crosses used as pendants, four wristbands two of which are stamped "Montreal" and one of which bears the mark of Robert Cruickshank, a star brooch made by Jonas Schindler, an engraved circular brooch, an engraved ear wheel, two large ornate brooches one of which is marked "Montreal," and four gorgets. One of these, a large circular gorget marked "Montreal," has the figure of a running fox engraved upon its face (Fig. 29, F). A large crescent-shaped gorget marked "New York" has the figure of a raccoon engraved upon its face (Fig. 29, A). Two smaller crescent-shaped gorgets without maker's marks have engravings — one a turtle, the other a European conventionalized symbol of the sun with a face in it.

About 175 glass beads were found with the dead. Most of these were translucent, multifaceted, cut glass beads that were light blue, dark blue, green, or colorless. These ranged from $\frac{3}{16}$ to $\frac{5}{16}$ inch in length and $\frac{2}{16}$ to $\frac{4}{16}$ inch in diameter. There were many spheroidal and oblate spheroidal beads in opaque black, blue, or pink and in translucent greens and blues. Sizes of these beads range from $\frac{2}{16}$ to $\frac{7}{16}$ inch in length and from $\frac{3}{16}$ to $\frac{6}{16}$ inch in diameter.

The assemblage of trade goods found with the burials at this site is typical of the Late Historical period. The presence of trade silver ornaments made by Cruickshank and Schindler indicates a date more recent than 1775. The probable date is sometime between 1775 and 1820.

Along the St. Joseph River in or near Niles, Michigan, there have been found from time to time various datable remains that must certainly be those of Potawatomi Indians who inhabited such villages as those of Cheenango, Moccasin, Koassun, and Matchkee (see Tucker, 1942, map 48). On the river bluff near Niles in 1952 there were found two burials and a number of trade objects

Fig. 29. — Some engravings on silver gorgets and armbands typical of the Late Historic period, 1760–1820. Courtesy of Chicago Natural History Museum. Examples show real (A, E, F) and mythical (D, L) animals; native (G, H, I, J, K,) and European (C) styles of design; and geometric design (B).

representative of the Late Historic period. I examined this find in the Fort St. Joseph Museum at Niles in the summer of 1963. Adhering to one of the skulls there was a fragmentary piece of trade cloth to which were attached about twenty-five or thirty small round brooches of silver so closely spaced or overlapping as to produce an appearance not unlike that of chain mail. Among the other items of trade there were two silver armbands, one of which bore the mark of Robert Cruickshank of Montreal, a crescent-shaped gorget, also made by Cruickshank, upon which was engraved a horned owl, a similar silver gorget upon which was engraved a running wolf, two silver ear wheels, an earring of silver, and an iron strike-a-light for making fire.

Another burial in Niles, on top of the bluff above the St. Joseph River, was excavated in 1958 (see Jelinek, 1958). The burial was that of a woman about twenty-three years old interred in a wooden coffin made of planks held together with square nails of forged iron. The position of the skeleton showed that the woman had been placed in the coffin on her back with her hands together in the area of the pubic arch. The coffin had been buried in an east-west position, with the head toward the west. Silver ornaments found with this burial consisted of thirty-nine small round brooches, two similar brooches with ornate rims, ten small but ornate crosses of the single-barred variety, two small. pendants one of which was serrated, some beads of tubular form, a hair pipe 1½ inches long, six earbobs, and five spoon-shaped lockets. One of these, when cleaned, showed the maker's stamp of Robert Cruickshank. Other ornaments were some small tubular beads of dark opaque glass ¼ inch long and some small spheroidal beads ⅛ inch in diameter made of dark-colored opaque glass. Impressions of fabric and hair and the positions of some ornaments indicate that, when placed in the coffin, the young Indian woman had her hair in braids, was clothed in trade cloth ornamented with small round brooches of silver, and wore a necklace of silver spoon lockets and crosses. The assemblage of trade goods shows that burial took place in the Late Historic period and probably in the latter half of the period.

Not far from Niles, on the north side of Dowagiac Creek, about one mile east of its junction with the St. Joseph River, there was a burial site excavated in 1935 (see Quimby, 1938, p. 68). One

grave contained the skeleton of an adult Indian in a semiflexed
position. At the feet of the skeleton there was a large brass pot
with an iron bail, and in the left hand of the skeleton there was
a tobacco pipe of polished stone. Near-by was another grave, containing the skeleton of a child buried with two brass hawk bells,
a large iron spoon, and a number of small round brooches of
silver. The pipe of polished stone was of native manufacture but
patterned after a style of European kaolin pipe obtained in trade.
The bowl was slightly curved, joined to the short stem at an oblique
angle, and had a short spar at its base; the plane of the lip of the
bowl was nowhere near parallel to the stem. In brief, the trade
pipe that was the model for this stone pipe possessed attributes
that suggest the Middle Historic period. On the other hand, the
near-by grave of the child contained silver ornaments indicative
of the Late Historic period. If the graves are contemporaneous or
nearly so, these burials probably date from the beginning of the
Late Historic period, *circa* 1760.

The Ottawa

There are some sites of the Late Historic period that we can assume are Ottawa because they are in areas known to have been inhabited only by the Ottawa at the time indicated by the trade
objects found in these sites. One such site was at the junction of
the Thornapple and Grand rivers, near Ada, in Kent County,
Michigan (see Herrick, 1958). This site and its contents have been
described and analyzed by Dr. Ruth Herrick, who salvaged materials and information from a burial ground that had been dis-
turbed by removal of soil for use in gardening. Accompanying the
burials of children and adults there were tools, utensils, weapons,
and ornaments that had been obtained through channels of trade
with white men. Except in the case of one extended burial it was
not possible to determine the positions of the skeletons prior to
their disturbance, nor was it possible to determine the specific associations between skeletons and artifacts. Included among these
artifacts were iron knives, some with decorative handles of perforated brass, an iron axe, a tomahawk pipe of iron, strike-a-lights
of iron, dark-colored gunflints with square heels, brass cooking
pots with covers, wooden spoons of native manufacture, fragments
of cloth from clothing and blankets, brass thimbles, a small rec-

tanguloid glass bottle labeled "Essence of Peppermint," and a small fiddle-shaped bottle that had once contained "Turlington's Balsom [sic] of Life."

There were also ornaments of silver and beads of glass with these burials. The silver ornaments included a number of earbobs; an ear wheel made by Robert Cruickshank of Montreal; four or five wristbands, one of which was marked "Montreal"; a broken arm-band; many fragments of small and miniature crosses of both double- and single-barred types, one of which was made by John Oaks of Montreal and another of which was made by Robert Cruickshank; two medium-sized double-barred crosses, one of them bearing the mark of Charles Arnoldi of Montreal; a single-barred cross of medium size made by Arnoldi; a number of small round brooches; four heart-shaped brooches made by Robert Cruickshank; a large ornate brooch made by A. and J. Scrymgeour of New York; and two smaller brooches made by Montreal silversmiths.

Twenty varieties of trade beads were found, including glass seed beads and commercial shell or wampum beads. Those diagnostic of the Late Historic period (or perhaps, its latter half) were multifaceted cut glass beads of transparent or translucent blues and opal; round beads of transparent green, amber, or colorless glass; tubular beads of opaque black or light transparent blue glass (in imitation of manufactured shell wampum); large round polka dot or "eyed" beads of opaque black or dark blue with opaque yellow and white or blue and red dots; and a few large and elegant oval beads of transparent green with wreath designs in yellow that encircled their mid-sections.

The trade objects associated with these Ottawa burials are clearly indicative of the Late Historic period, especially the latter half. I would suspect the main occupancy of this site have been between 1790 and 1820.

Another site in Ottawa territory was located in the Thornapple River Valley of Kent County, Michigan, in Cascade Township (see Quimby, 1938, pp. 67–68). In a grave with the skeleton of a young adult female there were some small spheroidal beads of white opaque glass, a small brass kettle, iron scissors, a strike-a-light of iron, some small round brooches of silver, a double-barred cross of silver, a long, flat, curved bone needle for making mats, and an iron awl with a bone handle decorated with an incised zig-zag design. The trade objects and location of the site are indicative of Ottawa Indian culture of the Late Historic period.

Not far from the mouth of the Kalamazoo River in Allegan County, Michigan, an extensive Indian cemetery was found in 1929 within the town limits of Saugatuck. Between thirty and fifty burials were encountered during excavation work for the construction of a new community hall. About fifteen of the skeletons were reported to have been in a flexed or partly flexed position. Others apparently were extended, but unfortunately the record is incomplete. In 1937, I examined a collection of materials found in the graves and still in the possession of the city of Saugatuck. There were numerous fragments of birch bark, probably the remains of bark sheets used to line the grave pits. There were also many bundles of feathers tied with cloth strips. Perhaps these were religious offerings of some kind or parts of medicine bundles. Tools and utensils included six brass kettles, fragments of pewter porringers, an iron butcher knife with a wooden handle, at least four iron axes, an iron strike-a-light, one pair of brass-rimmed spectacles, a small ovate mirror of glass, several silver spoons both large and small, and some fragments of Staffordshire style chinaware with a transfer design in deep, mottled blue. Fragments of cloth included silk, cotton prints, and heavy woolens of the thickness of a blanket. There were two kaolin trade pipes, a white pipe of porcelain-like material with a metal top, and a carved wooden pipe with a crudely inserted brass lining that probably was of native manufacture.

A large number of silver ornaments had been found with the burials. There were numerous miniature round brooches, some of which were still attached to cloth in rows or in areas solidly filled with brooches. There were six large silver armbands, upon some of which were engraved United States eagles after the style of Charles A. Burnett, an American silversmith; six circular gorgets, some with animals engraved upon them; a silver hatband; two circular ornate brooches; and two crescent-shaped gorgets, one of which had the American eagle engraved upon its face. The silver ornaments thus far listed had no discernible maker's marks, although such might have come to light had the silver been cleaned. There were, however, three pieces that were marked. One of these was a large single-barred silver cross with the touchmark "JK" in a square cartouche, probably made by John Kinzie who engaged in the manufacture of silver ornaments from 1780 to 1812 and is better known as an early resident of Chicago. The other two pieces are silver bracelets, one made probably by Narcisse Roy of Montreal and the other bearing an unidentified Canadian mark consisting of the script letters "WC" in a curvilinear cartouche. The Kinzie mark or the presence of the United States eagle motifs on silver suggests a date around 1812 or later for the old Indian cemetery in Saugatuck. The Indians who occupied the Saugatuck area at this time were generally Ottawa, although there may have been mixed settlements of Potawatomi and Ottawa.

The lower Grand River Valley of western Michigan was occupied by Ottawa Indians in the latter half of the Late Historic period, and there were three or four villages along the river in Ottawa County. A cemetery site in this locality may have served these villages or perhaps a later mixed settlement of Ottawa and Potawatomi dating from 1830 to the 1850's. In 1955, when the Grand River was cutting into the edge of this cemetery, Mr. George Davis and Mr. Edward Gillis of Grand Rapids salvaged some skeletons and a quantity of burial furniture from the site. In 1963, Mr. Davis and Mr. Gillis kindly allowed me to study the materials they had excavated there and to photograph selected samples. The skeletons were buried in an extended position, some of them in wooden boxes or coffins.

Artifacts of native manufacture or partly of native manufacture consisted of a wooden ladle-like spoon, some fragments of animal skin upon which were fastened white and blue seed beads of glass arranged in a curvilinear pattern, probably a floral design, and some strips of silver cut from a gorget or armband obtained from traders. On one of these strips there is engraved a raccoon-like animal, and upon another is what appears to be a word "Cenwis" in script.

Among the silver ornaments from this site are a large ornate pierced brooch still attached to a fragment of heavy cloth, an ear wheel that has been converted into a brooch by the addition of a hinged pin, eleven ornate pierced brooches of medium size, a strip of grosgrain ribbon with three miniature round brooches fastened to it, four medium-sized round brooches with wide rims and curvilinear zigzags engraved on them, five small round brooches, three earbobs, a long silver tube like a hair pipe or a feather-holder, and two small single-barred crosses, one of which displays the maker's stamp of Robert Cruickshank. There were also an armband and three bracelets, one of which was still around the lower armbones of an adult Indian.

Some other trade objects were a shallow pan of iron, three brass thimbles, a fragmentary butcher knife with an openwork brass handle fitted over a wooden core, an iron butcher knife with a wooden handle, two brass or bronze frames for jew's-harps, a medicine vial of glass, an iron dagger or sheath knife with wooden fragments of the handle, a pewter spoon, six prismatic gunflints of gray color, one honey-colored gunflint of the round-heel spall type, an iron strike-a-light of C-shaped form, a broad-bladed chisel, a molded flask of greenish glass with a cornucopia design in low relief, two china bowls of Staffordshire type with transfer designs, one in mottled blue, the other in light brown, and a small effigy pipe of fired clay. This pipe is an equal-arm elbow type with short stem and is blue to brown in color. The bowl is in the form of a human head wearing a turban and facing away from the smoker.

Glass beads found with these burials consisted of small multi-faceted types of very dark blue, large multifaceted types of translucent blue, green, and lavender, large wound or coiled beads of white or light green colors, round beads of apple red, spheroidal and barrel-shaped beads of translucent amber glass, large round or pear-shaped forms of translucent greenish glass, and fairly large barrel-shaped polychrome beads of bluish green with white floral or leaf motifs encircling the mid-sections.

The trade goods associated with these burials suggest a date in the latter half of the Late Historic period and probably even somewhat later. I estimated that this cemetery embraces a span of time from around 1810 to 1830. The Ottawa who settled along the Grand River had come there from L'Arbre Croche sometime in the first half of the Late Historic period.

L'Arbre Croche was the name given to the area along the shore of Lake Michigan between Waugoshance Point and Petoskey, in Emmet County, Michigan. It was a principal village of the Ottawas from A.D. 1742, and there are still Ottawa living in the area

at the present time, particularly at Cross Village. This area, therefore, should be the ideal locality for archaeological investigations
of Ottawa culture as it was in the Late Historic period. Unfortunately there has not been excavation of professional caliber undertaken in the area. Some burials excavated from a sandy ridge
south of Cross Village between 1875 and 1900 produced large
quantities of silver ornaments, most of which were made in Montreal between 1780 and 1810, some multifaceted glass beads of
several colors, three brass pots, and several fragments of cloth.
The only artifacts of native manufacture were a carved wooden
spoon, a small ovoid bowl of carved wood, a broken gorget of
marine shell, five square beads of thin catlinite, and a small skin
bag filled with powdered vermilion (see Quimby, 1938, p. 66).
A somewhat similar group of burials and associated trade objects
poorly excavated in 1897–1900 from a site in the same general
area has been described and analyzed by Dr. Robert C. Alberts
(1953, pp. 89–95). Both series of burials probably are representative of Ottawa culture at about the period of the War
of 1812.

The Menomini

The following information about a Menomini burial was gener-
ously given to me by Dr. Robert L. Hall, Curator of Anthropology
at Illinois State Museum. About 1935 a burial was encountered
by excavators preparing the foundation of an industrial building
in Green Bay, Wisconsin, at the site of the "Old King's Village,"
an historic Menomini settlement of which one of Dr. Hall's ances-
tors had been chief. This burial consisted of the skeleton of an
adult Indian accompanied by an iron axe, a necklace, and a number of silver ornaments. The necklace was composed of fifty or
more tubular beads of rolled brass or copper (probably brass),
two glass seed beads, and an ovoid pendant of stone. The silver
ornaments were as follows: a circular gorget $3\frac{3}{4}$ inches in diameter, made by Jonas Schindler of Quebec, upon which was engraved a flying goose (Fig. 29, E), an armband $2\frac{1}{2}$ inches wide,
made by Robert Cruickshank of Montreal, upon which was engraved an elaborate cruciform design (Fig. 29, B); an armband
$1\frac{7}{8}$ inches wide, made by Jonas Schindler, upon which was engraved a bird like a turkey (Fig. 29, G); a similar armband made

by the same silversmith upon which was engraved a similar bird in a different pose (Fig. 29, K); and two bracelets ½ inch wide and ⅝ inch wide made by Robert Cruickshank. These artifacts are in the collection of the Neville Public Museum. The silver ornaments such as the armbands and the gorget suggest the skeleton was that of a male, and the trade goods viewed as a group indicate to me that the burial took place between 1780 and 1810. However, a male Indian, buried in such fine apparel as silver armbands, bracelets, gorget, and a necklace of brass beads should have had more than just an iron axe with him in his grave. Probably some additional items were missed by the construction workers who made the discovery.

Another Menomini or possibly a Winnebago site about 45 miles south of Green Bay at Butte des Morts, Wisconsin, was discovered by sewer-diggers in the spring of 1930 (see Overton, 1931, pp. 91–97). Two burials of the Late Historic period were removed from this location. One grave contained the extended skeleton of an adult male with his head oriented in the direction of the setting sun. Associated with this burial were the following silver ornaments: an armband made by Cruickshank, upon which was engraved a mythical underwater monster; another armband with an eaglelike bird engraved upon it; a circular gorget made by Charles Arnoldi of Montreal, upon which was engraved a swanlike bird; a double heart and crown brooch made by Cruickshank; a quadrilateral brooch made by Cruickshank; a hollow boat-shaped pendant; an ear ornament made by Cruickshank with three small crosses dangling from it; two large earbobs; two finger rings; and more than 150 small circular brooches. There were also 200 small white seed beads of glass and a few small tubular beads of glass or shell, four large metal buttons, and eight large tubular beads of bone, which were found near the skull and may have been part of a head ornament. What probably was part of a sacred medicine bag consisted of a pouch of some sort of fine-grained skin with a trace of vermilion near it, a flint arrowhead painted with vermilion, and a flint scraper similarly painted. These antique flints probably had been picked up and preserved for their assumed magical properties.

Some fifteen cone-shaped tinklers found with this burial were made of sheet brass from worn out kettles. They had tufts of hair in their large openings and probably adorned a shirt. Tools and weapons found with this burial include a catlinite pipe, a fragmentary bone awl, an iron butcher knife, an iron axe, an iron strike-a-light of oval shape, a large iron spear point or club blade 8 inches long, two gunflints, and a flintlock pistol.

The second grave contained the extended skeleton of a woman also oriented with head to the west. With this burial was an oval iron strike-a-light, two fire flints of native manufacture, parts of a round metal box, and a small metal-backed mirror. Ornaments with the skeleton consisted of seventy-eight white seed beads of glass, some hundreds of small tubular beads (wampum) of shell or glass, and a number of silver ornaments. These were as follows: two small double-barred crosses made by Robert Cruickshank of Montreal; two large double-barred crosses; four or more quadrilateral brooches; two bracelets, one made by Cruickshank; two flattened halves of bracelets, one of which had the mark of Jonas Schindler stamped on it; a portion of a spoon locket; a number of earbobs; three tinkling cones made of sheet silver cut from other ornaments; and 119 small round brooches.

Most of the materials found with the two skeletons at Butte des Morts are now in the Oshkosh Public Museum. The trade goods are typical of the Late Historic period and probably of the middle portion, say 1780 to 1800.

THE CHIPPEWA

The Chippewa, as a vast, loose tribal entity, came into being in the Late Historic period, the result of a process of fusion of closely related peoples, a process that had been in operation since the early days of the fur trade. By the beginning of the Late Historic period in 1760 organized activity in Chippewa social, political, and economic realms was vested in village units, whereas in earlier times among the proto-Chippewa such activities were vested in totemic kin groups (see Hickerson, 1962, pp. 87–88). Some village (Fig. 30) and cemetery sites of the Chippewa in the period from 1760 to 1820 are described in the following pages.

In the southwestern part of Escanaba, Michigan, on the sandy bluff overlooking the waters of northern Green Bay, a burial was accidentally encountered in 1901 during construction of a house. This burial must have been Chippewa because they were the Indians occupying that particular area in the Late Historic period and the burial dates from that time. In the sandy grave there was the skeleton of an adult Indian, and with it there were a number of artifacts which are now in the Escanaba Historical Museum, where I examined them in the summer of 1963. One was a Dakota (Sioux) style elbow pipe of gray stone about 7 inches long, with a crenulated ridge along the upper side of the stem. Probably this pipe was attached to a long and elaborate wooden stem which disintegrated in the grave. There were two fragments of trade cloth, to which were fastened rows of small white beads (seed beads) of glass. A hundred or so of these beads found in the grave probably were once fastened to sashes or garters of woven trade yarns. Silver ornaments consisted of an ornate triple-barred cross about 7 inches long stamped with the mark of Jonas Schindler, a Canadian silversmith, an ear wheel with a star motif, and a large ornate brooch about 6 inches in diameter. Some other objects in the grave were an oval mirror, a brass thimble converted into a tinkler, a large brass ring that probably was a neck ornament, a small glass medicine bottle or vial about 6 inches high,

Fig. 30. — Chippewa Indian encampment in Lake Superior area during the Late Historic period, 1760–1820. Courtesy of Chicago Natural History Museum.

and a device for removing facial hair by pulling it out. This Indian shaving kit consisted of a short wooden rod on which was a section of closely coiled spring of brass wire. To remove hair the coils were spread, then pushed together to grip the hair, which was then pulled out. It was a kind of multiple tweezers. One of these objects collected from Fox Indians in 1896 is shown in Figure 31, *top left*. Luckily the Indians did not have much facial hair anyway.

One of the principal settlements of the Chippewa during the Late Historic period was on Madeline Island, a part of northernmost Wisconsin in Lake Superior. The Chippewa had first settled there in large numbers during the Middle Historic period, which was their "golden age" in this particular area. But the Chippewa continued on in their Chequamegon or La Pointe village throughout the Late Historic period, and some Chippewa are still living in the area today. From time to time artifacts and various materials representative of the Chippewa in the Late Historic period are found in the locus of the old settlement on Madeline Island. A considerable collection of these items has been excavated by Mr. Al Galazen of La Pointe.

The Chippewa material from the site on Madeline Island is unusually well preserved because it is found beneath the water table. Yet at the time of deposition or burial the particular places that relate to the Chippewa occupancy must have been above the

Fig. 31. — Some artifacts of the Late Historic period, 1760–1820. Courtesy of Chicago Natural History Museum. *Top left*: a hair-puller consisting of brass coil on wooden holder. *Bottom left*: stone pipe from Madeline Island. *Center*: Iroquois pipe of stone. *Right*: strike-a-light of steel.

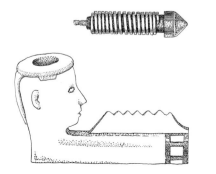

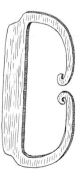

water table. The reason for this is that the north shore of Lake Superior has been slowly rising for some thousands of years and is still being upwarped. Since the whole Lake Superior basin is involved in the tilting and since the north shore is rising faster than the south shore the latter is subject to drowning. The effect is about the same as if the south shore were sinking. This means that areas that were land a hundred or more years ago have been washed into Lake Superior and are now under water, and it means that existing land that was above the water table 150 or 200 years ago is now beneath the water table.

In 1961 and again in 1963, I was graciously allowed to study the Chippewa materials excavated from Madeline Island. A part of this collection was in the possession of Mr. Galazen and part was in the Madeline Island Historical Museum at La Pointe. Relics of the Late Historic period Chippewa occupancy of Madeline Island include the usual silver ornaments made by Canadian silversmiths and numerous parts of flintlock guns such as dragon or serpent sideplates of cast brass, barrels with octagonal butt sections, iron and brass butt plates, lock plates and dark gray gunflints of prismatic form with squared heel. There were also sherds of Staffordshire-like china, pewter dishes and porringers or fragments of these, spoons of pewter and silver, two-tined forks with bone handles bearing an incised hachure design, a "By the King's Patent Essence of Peppermint" bottle, an ovoid silver box with a fish engraved on the lid, and two glass bottle necks with double lip bands at their tops. Some additional trade objects were oval mirrors of glass, iron strike-a-lights of oval and C-shaped styles (Fig. 31), brass thimbles, some of which were used as tinklers, two brass openwork handles for butcher knives, a jackknife with a wooden handle, scissors, wrought iron nails, butcher knife blades, iron axes, fragments of cloth, numerous fragments of white kaolin pipes, and a hair remover consisting of a brass coil spring over a wooden dowel.

Objects of native manufacture included a crude human effigy carved of wood, which probably was a kind of fertility medicine; part of the bow or stern of a birchbark canoe; a section of birch bark with tightly sewn seams, probably part of a rogan or storage box; a large birchbark sheet with the outline of a two-masted

schooner engraved upon it; numerous rolls of birch bark in assorted lengths and widths, many of them tied with grass strings;
several kinds of stone pipes to be described presently; a fragment
of a woolen sash or garter of dark wool decorated with small white
beads of glass that form in outline a pattern of conjoined squares
arranged in parallel zigzags; a flat oval stone with incised cross-
hatching; and two small bundles wrapped in cylinders of sheet
silver. The smaller of the two, about 1¼ inches high by 1 inch
in diameter, consists of a cylinder of sheet silver cut from a
bracelet or armband held by lacings around a tubular bundle of
organic material. The larger of the two, about 3¾ inches high
by 1½ inches in diameter, consists of a similar cylinder made
from part of a silver armband wrapped around a bundle of organic material.

There were several styles of stone tobacco pipes of native manufacture. Most common was a variant of the Micmac style consisting of a short tulip-shaped bowl on a blocklike base into which
was inserted a short wooden stem. Some pipes of this style had a
short perforated keel at the bottom of the base. A fiber cord or
leather thong through the hole in the keel held the pipe to the
stem. This style of pipe was still in use in the twentieth century
in the forests north of Lake Superior and was derived from a
somewhat similar but larger Micmac pipe that appeared in the
Middle Historic period and which may have been made especially
for the fur trade in the upper Great Lakes region. Another style
of pipe excavated from the occupation layers of Late Historic period Chippewa on Madeline Island is the calumet, derived from
Dakota (Siouan people). Pipes in this category are elbow-shaped
and made of catlinite and other stone, and often ornamented with
geometric designs of inlaid lead. These pipes usually had long
wooden stems that were decorated elaborately. One calumet-style
pipe with lead inlay in its hexagonal base was made of whitish
stone and had a bowl carved in the form of a human head with
face toward the stem. The hair of the effigy formed a single braid
at the back of the pipe bowl, and a realistic ear was carved on
each side; this pipe resembles an Iroquois style that was still in
use in the nineteenth century (see Fig. 31). Another calumet-like
elbow pipe of gray stone had a hexagonal base or stem section

and a bowl that was hexagonal in its lower half and bulbous in its upper half. At the end of the base where the wooden stem would be inserted there was a band of decoration consisting of three incised lines bordered by rows of small shallow holes. There are paired incised lines on the upper three facets of the hexagonal base.

The glass trade beads found in the Chippewa occupation layers of the Late Historic period on Madeline Island were of those styles typical of the period. There were two hundred or more small white glass beads of the kind known as seed beads; some one hundred or so assorted seed beads of blue, black, and red glass; about one hundred multifaceted blue glass beads of medium size; about twenty-five similar beads of translucent clear glass; and five spheroidal beads of blue opaque glass. Not only these glass beads but also the silver ornaments and other trade objects just mentioned are representative of the Late Historic period and thus date this particular occupation of Madeline Island to a time between 1760 and 1820. Abundant documentary evidence indicates that a division of the Chippewa occupied the island at that time.

SUMMARY

This brief survey of archaeological samples from the Indian cultures of the Late Historic period shows that by 1760 or shortly afterwards the Indians of the upper Great Lakes region had discarded most of their material culture in favor of new things introduced by the fur traders, so that a kind of Pan-Indian culture had emerged. The Indians manifesting this culture made their living hunting and trapping. Their principal product was beaver fur, which they exchanged for tools, weapons, utensils, ornaments, food, liquor, and other things supplied by traders.

The historical documentation available for the Late Historic period makes it possible as a rule to determine what tribe of Indians was associated with a given assemblage of archaeological remains. In this chapter I have discussed findings at sites associated with the Sauk, the Fox, the Potawatomi, the Ottawa, the Menomini, and the Chippewa. The Chippewa are of particular significance, as having come into being, by a process of fusion, during the Late Historic period. The final chapter takes a more leisurely look at the Chippewa culture.

References

Alberts, 1953; Herrick, 1958; Hewitt, 1912; Hickerson, 1962; Jelinek, 1958; Overton, 1931; Quimby, 1938; Tucker, 1942.

CHAPTER 11

ARCHAEOLOGY AND ETHNOLOGY
OF A CHIPPEWA FAMILY
IN THE LATE HISTORIC PERIOD

Introduction

What were Indian cultures and societies really like in the Late Historic period? Although it is possible to make meaningful reconstructions from the data of archaeology alone, it frequently happens that a greater amount of information can be obtained from the firsthand observations of an early traveler, priest, or trader who kept a diary or records of some sort. Such persons can become unintentional historians and ethnologists as viewers or even participant viewers of what were once functioning cultures and societies that became extinct long before the advent of trained ethnologists and archaeologists. And although their observations were fragmentary and their records incomplete, the written accounts of travelers, priests, and traders are exceedingly important because there is nothing better in place of them. From the record of one of these unintentional ethnologists, Alexander Henry, comes an illuminating view of Indian life in the Late Historic period.

The travels and adventures of Alexander Henry, a well-known

English fur trader of the late eighteenth century, were first published in 1809. In Henry's work there are a number of personal observations of the Chippewa that can provide useful data for the archaeologist and the ethnohistorian. It is possible, for instance, to reconstruct in considerable part the annual pattern of subsistence activities and social life of the somewhat acculturated Chippewa who lived in northern Michigan in 1763–64, and thereby obtain a concept of a part of Chippewa tribal culture as it existed in the latter half of the eighteenth century.

Alexander Henry survived the Indian massacre of the English at Fort Michilimackinac in early June of 1763 because he had been adopted as a brother, or perhaps a son, by a Chippewa Indian named Wawatam. Although prior to this time Henry had lived somewhat like an Indian, for the next twelve months he lived *as* an Indian. About June 9, 1763, Henry and the Wawatam family went to Mackinac Island from Fort Michilimackinac. From there they went to "the Bay of Boutchitaouy" (St. Martin Bay) and then to St. Martin Island, both in northern Lake Huron, where they remained until August 20, 1763. The Wawatam family next returned to Fort Michilimackinac, where they obtained necessary supplies, and then journeyed down the west coast of Michigan to the mouth of the river Aux Sables, somewhere between Big and Little Point Sable, Michigan. In December 1763 the Wawatam family and Henry traveled into north central Michigan in the area between the Manistee and Muskegon rivers and south of Cadillac, Michigan. They were about 60 or 70 miles inland from Lake Michigan (Quimby, 1962). Here they remained until March 1764 and then returned to a sugaring place not far from the Lake Michigan shore. At the beginning of April they returned to the border of Lake Michigan, and by the end of April 1764 they were back at Fort Michilimackinac. In early May they went to St. Martin Bay to fish and to hunt wild fowl. Sometime near the middle of May 1764, Henry took leave of the Wawatam family and went north to Sault Ste Marie.

THE FAMILY

The Chippewa family of which Alexander Henry was a member by adoption consisted of Wawatam, who was "master of the family"; Wawatam's wife; the eldest son of Wawatam; this son's wife

and baby born in the summer of 1763; the younger son of Wawatam; and Wawatam's thirteen-year-old daughter, who would have
been considered an adult by Indian standards (Henry, ed. Bain,
1901, pp. 110, 114). There was thus a family group composed of
four adult males, three adult females, and one infant, a total of
eight persons. This family provided an effective work force of
seven people.

CLOTHING

Alexander Henry was dressed by the Wawatam family so that he
would look like a typical Chippewa of the time and place (Fig.
32). He describes his own appearance in these words (Henry, ed.
Bain, 1901, pp. 111–12):

My hair was cut off, and my head shaved, with the exception of a spot
on the crown, of about twice the diameter of a crown-piece [coin]. My
face was painted with three or four different colours; some parts of it
red, and others black. A shirt was provided for me, painted with ver-
million, mixed with grease. A large collar of wampun was put around
my neck, and another suspended on my breast. Both my arms were decorated with large bands of silver above the elbow, besides several smaller
ones on the wrists; and my legs were covered with *mitasses* [leggings], a
kind of hose, made, as is the favorite fashion, of scarlet cloth. Over all,
I was to wear a scarlet blanket or mantle, and on my head a large bunch
of feathers. I parted, not without some regret, with the long hair which
was natural to it, and which I fancied to be ornamental; but the ladies of the
family, and of the village, in general, appeared to think my person im-
proved, and now condescended to call me handsome, even among Indians.

Upon Henry's return to Fort Michilimackinac in late April of
1764 and while he was still living as an Indian, he purchased two
shirts, a pair of leggings of scarlet cloth with ribbon to garnish
them, and a blanket.

SHELTER

Alexander Henry does not supply enough information for an adequate description of Chippewa types of shelters. He refers to
houses, lodges, wigwams, and cabins. In one place he describes
a rectangular house 20 feet long and 14 feet wide with a door at
each end, a continuous fireplace running down the middle of the
house from one end to the other, and a smoke hole above it (Henry,
ed. Bain, 1901, p. 70). This house held eight persons and was

Fig. 32. — Alexander Henry dressed as an Indian after his capture by Chippewa in 1763. Courtesy of Chicago Natural History Museum.

built in one day. Elsewhere Henry mentions a lodge holding four-teen prisoners, "tied two and two, with each a rope about his neck, and made fast to a pole which might be called the supporter of the building" (Henry, ed. Bain, 1901, p. 97). These fragmentary bits of evidence suggest a kind of rectangular cabin with gabled roof made of poles and covered with slabs of bark. Such dwellings seem to have been common in much of the upper Great Lakes region in the eighteenth century and probably were of composite origin, derived mainly from the Huron long-houses and the French peasant's cabin. On other grounds it seems likely that the Chippewa of this period also used conical and dome-shaped wigwams, but Henry does not give any evidence of this.

Travel and Transportation

In spring, summer, and autumn the Chippewa traveled in birch-bark canoes. In winter they traveled on foot, aided by snowshoes when the snow was deep on the ground.

The birchbark canoes ranged in size from those about 12 feet long to large freight canoes 35 to 40 feet long, which required a crew of about fourteen men and could carry 6,000 pounds or more in addition to the crew. Alexander Henry and his Chippewa friends probably used canoes that were about 15 feet long.

On land, burdens were carried on a person's back with the aid of a burden strap across the forehead. Much of this kind of transport was done by the women.

Time, Place, and Subsistence

In the summer of 1763 the Wawatam family and Alexander Henry made their living by hunting wild fowl and fishing. They left Mackinac Island, partly because of scarcity of food there, some-time in the latter half of June 1763 and moved via canoe to St. Martin Bay. Somewhere along the shore of this bay they estab-lished a lodge large enough to accommodate seven adults. After the birth of Wawatam's grandchild, they took residence on St. Martin Island. Of this sojourn on St. Martin Island, Henry writes, "Our object was to fish for sturgeon, which we did with great suc-cess; and here, in the enjoyment of a plentiful and excellent sup-ply of food, we remained until the twentieth day of August" (Henry, ed. Bain, 1901, p. 121). The sturgeon has an average weight of

60 pounds and a maximum of 150 pounds (Hinsdale, 1932, p. 16).

The autumn being at hand, or so considered, in late August of 1763 the Wawatam family and Henry prepared to go to Wawatam's wintering-ground. "At our wintering-ground," Henry remarks, "we were to be alone; for the Indian families, in the countries of which I write, separate in the winter season, for the convenience, as well of subsistence as of the chase, and re-associate in the spring and summer" (Henry, ed. Bain, 1901, p. 122). Accordingly they left St. Martin Island and went by canoe to Fort Michilimackinac where they obtained from a trader on credit "some trifling articles, together with ammunition, and two bushels of maize."

This done, Wawatam, with his family and Henry, steered directly for Lake Michigan. At the Ottawa village of L'Arbre Croche at the northwestern tip of the Lower Peninsula of Michigan the group stopped for one day, and an Ottawa chief gave Henry a bag of maize. "It is the Ottawas, it will be remembered, who raise this grain, for the market of Michilimackinac," Henry notes (Henry, ed. Bain, 1901, p. 122). Unless the Wawatam family obtained more maize than Henry recorded, their total supply for the coming winter was two bushels and one bag (of perhaps 50 pounds). As already noted, the family, including Alexander Henry, consisted of seven adults and one nursing infant.

Leaving L'Arbre Croche, the group journeyed by canoe southward along the western shore of the Lower Peninsula of Michigan to the mouth of the "river Aux Sables." On their way they killed many wild fowl and beaver.

To kill beaver [Henry writes] we used to go several miles up the rivers, before the approach of night, and after the dusk came on, suffer the canoe to drift gently down the current, without noise. The beaver in this part of the evening come abroad to procure food, or materials for repairing their habitations; and as they are not alarmed by the canoe, they often pass it within gun-shot. (Henry, ed. Bain, 1901, p. 123.)

Finally the Wawatam family reached its destination, and Henry relates that

On entering the river Aux Sables, Wawatam took a dog, tied its feet together, and threw it into the stream, uttering at the same time, a long prayer, which he addressed to the Great Spirit, supplicating his blessing on the chase, and his aid in the support of the family, through the dangers of a long winter. (Henry, ed. Bain, 1901, p. 123.)

The Wawatam family established its lodge 15 miles above the mouth of the river. At this encampment, or near-by, the family remained throughout the rest of the autumn. The principal animals of the region were the elk (Henry's term for elk is red-deer or stag), deer, bear, raccoon, beaver, and marten.

Raccoon-hunting was Alexander Henry's particular job during the autumn months. Before any snow had fallen, Henry and Wawatam's youngest son hunted raccoons in the evening, using dogs to tree the animals, after which they shot them.

After the falling of the snow [Henry observes] nothing more is necessary for taking the racoon, than to follow the track of his feet. . . . I have found six at a time in the hollow of one tree, lying upon each other, and nearly in a torpid state. . . .

. . . I usually went out at the first dawn of day, and seldom returned till sunset, or till I had laden myself with as many animals as I could carry. (Henry, ed. Bain, 1901, pp. 126–27.)

On the evening of November 1, 1763, when Alexander Henry returned from hunting, he found the Wawatam family preparing for a religious ritual. The fire in the lodge had been put out, the ashes removed, and "dry sand was spread where they had been." The smoke hole in the top of the lodge had been covered with skins "by this means excluding, as much as possible, external light." A fire was made outside "the cabin, in the open air, and a kettle hung over it to boil." Henry describes the ensuing ceremony as follows:

As soon as the darkness of night had arrived the family, including myself, were invited into the lodge. I was now requested not to speak, as a feast was about to be given to the dead, whose spirits delight in uninterrupted silence.

As we entered each was presented with his wooden-dish and spoon, after receiving which we seated ourselves. The door was next shut, and we remained in perfect darkness.

The master [Wawatam] of the family was the master of the feast. Still in the dark, he asked every one, by turn, for his dish, and put into each two boiled ears of maize. The whole being served, he began to speak. In his discourse, which lasted half an hour, he called upon the manes [spirits] of his deceased relations and friends, beseeching them to be present, to assist him in the chase, and to partake of the food which he had prepared for them. When he had ended, we proceeded to eat our maize, which we did without other noise than what was occasioned by our teeth. The maize was not half boiled, and it took me an hour to consume my share. I was requested not to break the spikes [cobs], as this would be displeasing to the departed spirits of their friends.

When all was eaten, Wawatam made another speech, with which the ceremony ended. A new fire was kindled, with fresh sparks, from flint and steel; and the pipes being smoked, the spikes were carefully buried, in a hole made in the ground for that purpose, within the lodge. This done, the whole family began a dance, Wawatam singing, and beating a drum. The dance continued the greater part of the night, to the great pleasure of the lodge. (Henry, ed. Bain, 1901, pp. 128–29.)

The Wawatam family continued to live in the same locale until after the middle of December 1763. Between the beginning of autumn and December 20 they acquired 100 beaver skins, at least 100 raccoon skins, and a "large quantity of dried venison; all of which was secured from the wolves, by being placed upon a scaffold" preparatory to the family's moving inland.

On December 21, 1763, Wawatam's group began its trek. Early in the morning "the bundles were made up by the women, for each person to carry." Henry notes that the bundle given him was the lightest and "those carried by the women, the largest and heaviest of the whole." On the first day the group marched about 20 miles and encamped. Wawatam killed an elk not far from the encampment and the next day the lodge was moved to the elk carcass; the latter probably weighed at least 600 pounds. Two days were spent at this location cutting elk meat into slices the thickness of a steak, and hanging these slices over the fire, in the smoke, to dry them. On the third day the family moved farther inland, marching until 2 o'clock in the afternoon, after which the three women in the group erected and prepared the lodges (Henry, ed. Bain, 1901, p. 130).

The Wawatam family was now inland from Lake Michigan some 60 or 70 miles in the pine forests somewhere between the Manistee and Muskegon rivers, probably in Osceola County, Michigan. Here they remained until March 1764, hunting beaver, elk, bear, and otter.

Elk seem to have been plentiful in the region. Henry encountered a herd of elk within two days of the time he arrived at the place of encampment in the interior of Michigan. February, the "Moon of Hard or Crusted Snow," was a month particularly suited for elk-hunting. Henry writes,

At this season, the stag [elk] is very successfully hunted, his feet breaking through at every step, and the crust upon the snow, cutting his legs, with its sharp edges, to the very bone. He is consequently, in this distress, an easy prey; and it frequently happened that we killed twelve in the short space of two hours. By this means, we were soon put into possession of four thousand [pounds] weight of dried venison. (Henry, ed. Bain, 1901, p. 139.)

A large number of beaver were taken by the Wawatam family in the winter of 1763–64. According to Henry,

The most common way of taking the beaver was that of breaking up its house, which is done with trenching-tools, during the winter, when the ice is strong enough to allow of approaching them; and when, also, the fur is in its most valuable state. Breaking up the house, however, is only a preparatory step. During this operation the [beaver] family made their escape to one or more of their *washes*. . . . From the washes, they must be taken out with the hands; and in doing this, the hunter sometimes receives severe wounds from their teeth. While a hunter, I thought, with the Indians, that the beaver-flesh was very good. (Henry, ed. Bain, 1901, p. 125.)

Sometime in January 1764 Alexander Henry discovered a bear in the hollow of a very large pine tree. This is Henry's account of the incident:

On returning to the lodge, I communicated my discovery; and it was agreed that all the family should go together in the morning, to assist in cutting down the tree, the girth of which was not less than three fathom [18 feet]. The women, at first opposed the undertaking, because our axes, being only of a pound and a half weight, were not well adapted to so heavy a labour; but, the hope of finding a large bear, and obtaining from its fat a great quantity of oil, an article at the time much wanted, at length prevailed.

Accordingly, in the morning, we surrounded the tree, both men and women, as many at a time as could conveniently work at it; and here we toiled, like beaver til the sun went down. This day's work carried us about half way through the trunk; and the next morning we renewed the attack, continuing it till about two o'clock, in the afternoon, when the tree fell to the ground. . . . there came out . . . a bear of extraordinary size which I shot. (Henry, ed. Bain, 1901, pp. 135–36.)

At this point the bear became the object of ceremonial activity on the part of the Wawatam family, after which the bear was cut up.

The skin being taken off, we found the fat in several places six inches deep. This, being divided into two parts, loaded two persons; and the flesh parts, were as much as four persons could carry. In all, the carcass must have exceeded five hundred [pounds] weight.

As soon as we reached the lodge, the bear's head was adorned with all the trinkets in the possession of the family, such as silver arm-bands and wrist-bands, and belts of wampum; and then laid upon a scaffold, set up for its reception, within the lodge. Near the nose was placed a large quantity of tobacco.

The next morning no sooner appeared, than preparations were made for a feast to the manes [spirits]. The lodge was cleaned and swept; and the head of the bear lifted up, and a new stroud blanket, which had never been used before, spread under it. The pipes were now lit: and Wawatam blew tobacco-smoke into the nostrils of the bear, telling me to do the same. (Henry, ed. Bain, 1901, p. 137.)

Following these ritual acts there was a ceremonial feast in which they "all ate heartily of the bear's flesh; and even the head itself, after remaining three days on the scaffold was put into the kettle."

The fat of [the] bear was melted down, and the oil filled six porcupine-skins. A part of the meat was cut into strips, and fire-dried, after which it was put into the vessels [porcupine skins] containing the oil, where it remained in perfect preservation, until the middle of summer. (Henry, ed. Bain, 1901, p. 139.)

By the latter part of February or early part of March 1764 it was time for the Wawatam family to move westward, back to the place from which they had departed the previous December 21. At this point, some 15 or more miles (the distance may depend upon which river Henry meant by Aux Sables) inland from Lake Michigan, they had left a cache of two hundred or more skins and a large quantity of dried venison. There were also stands of sugar maple trees in this area which the Wawatam family intended to exploit during the month of March.

There was a considerable quantity of luggage to be transported westward. In addition to blankets, cooking and eating utensils, guns, axes, and the like, there were furs and animal skins, six porcupine skins full of bear oil and strips of dried bear meat, some 4,000 pounds of dried venison, and one infant, all of which had to be carried by seven people. To do this the Wawatam family used a system of transport by stages which Henry describes in the following manner:

The women . . . prepared our loads; and the morning of departure being come, we sat [sic] off at daybreak, and continued our march until two o'clock in the afternoon. Where we stopped, we erected a scaffold, on which we deposited the bundles we had brought, and returned to our en-campment, which we reached in the evening. In the morning, we carried fresh loads, which being deposited with the rest, we returned [to our encampment] a second time in the evening. This we repeated, till all was forwarded one stage. Then, removing our lodge to the place of deposit, we carried our goods, with the same patient toil, a second stage; and so on, till we were at no great distance from the shores of the lake. . . . Arrived here, we turned our attention to sugar making, the management of which, as I have before related, belongs to the women, the men cutting wood for the fires, and hunting and fishing. (Henry, ed. Bain, 1901, pp. 141–42.)

What Henry had "before related" about the production of maple sugar had taken place the preceding March near Sault Ste Marie. At that place Henry and seven Chippewa Indians produced 1,600 pounds of maple sugar and 36 gallons of syrup in about one month. The eight people consumed 300 pounds of maple sugar during the month, and although, according to Henry, they hunted and fished, sugar was their principal food during this time (Henry, ed. Bain, 1901, pp. 70–71).

While the Wawatam family were at their sugaring place in the western part of the Lower Peninsula of Michigan they were joined by other Chippewa Indians. Henry says of this,

. . . we were joined by several lodges of Indians, most of whom were of the family [clan or band] to which I belonged, and had wintered near us. The lands belonged to this family [clan or band], and it had therefore the exclusive right to hunt on them. This is according to the custom of the people; for each family [clan or band] had its own lands. I was treated very civilly by all the lodges. (Henry, ed. Bain, 1901, p. 142.)

In the course of the sugaring operations a child (not of the Wawatam family) fell into a kettle of boiling syrup. While the child still lived there was continual ceremonial feasting, and as Henry reports,

Several sacrifices were also offered; among which were dogs, killed and hung upon the tops of poles, with the addition of stroud blankets and other articles. . . .

The child died. To preserve the body from the wolves, it was placed upon a scaffold, where it remained till we went to the lake [Lake Michigan], on the border of which was the burial-ground of the family.

On our arrival there, which happened in the beginning of April, I did not fail to attend the funeral. The grave was made of a large size, and the whole of the inside lined with birch-bark. On the bark was laid the body of the child, accompanied with an axe, a pair of snow-shoes, a small kettle, several pairs of common shoes, its own strings of beads, and — because it was a girl — a carrying-belt and a [canoe] paddle. The kettle was filled with meat.

All this was again covered with bark; and at about two feet nearer the surface, logs were laid across, and these again covered with bark, so that the earth might by no means fall upon the corpse. (Henry, ed. Bain, 1901, pp. 142–43.)

In April, while the Wawatam family and other Chippewa families were encamped on the border of Lake Michigan, Alexander Henry and about nineteen Indians went hunting for a "panther" (mountain lion or lynx) that had been seen in the vicinity. Henry says of this incident, "We had not proceeded more than a mile, before the dogs found the panther, and pursued him to a tree, on which he was shot. He was of a large size" (Henry, ed. Bain, 1901, pp. 145–46).

On April 25, 1764 the Wawatam family and the other Indians who had joined them near the Lake Michigan shore departed northward by canoe. On the south side of the opening into Grand Traverse Bay they encountered "a large party of Indians"; and from here "the united bands" journeyed to L'Arbre Croche and then on to Fort Michilimackinac, which they reached in the evening of April 27, 1764.

With one or both of the two French traders who were the only occupants of the Fort at this time, Wawatam and Henry settled their debts of the previous autumn. Henry's share of what remained after paying debts was a "hundred beaver-skins, sixty racoon-skins and six otter [skins], of the total value of about one hundred and sixty dollars" (Henry, ed. Bain, 1901, p. 147).

About May 6 the Wawatam family and Henry again went to St. Martin Bay, where they fished and hunted. About May 12, 1764, Alexander Henry took leave of the Wawatam family and went to Sault Ste Marie and resumed his life as a white man. Thus ended Alexander Henry's life as an Indian and his usefulness to this particular study.

ANALYSIS OF SUBSISTENCE

The only period in the year 1763–64 that Alexander Henry and the Wawatam family went hungry was in June of 1763, while they were living in the Chippewa village on Mackinac Island. Later in St. Martin Bay they lived on fish and wild fowl and still later on St. Martin Island they lived on a plentiful supply of sturgeon for the remainder of the summer.

In the autumn of 1763 they subsisted on maize they had received by purchase or gift and on beaver and raccoon flesh. They also had fish and wild fowl at this time. By December 20, 1763, the Wawatam family had taken one hundred beaver, at least one hundred raccoons, and enough elk or deer to produce a surplus of dried venison that was placed in a cache.

During the winter from December 1763 to March 1764 while in the interior of the Lower Peninsula of Michigan the Wawatam family had a plentiful supply of elk meat, not to mention beaver, otter, porcupine, and bear. By the end of the winter they had a temporary, at least, surplus of 4,000 pounds of dried venison and six porcupine skins of bear oil mixed with strips of bear meat. There is some suggestion that beaver and raccoon were common food items in autumn and early winter and that elk was most common in late winter. The bear the family secured seems to have been a kind of bonus or unexpected gift, valued primarily for its oil.

During March and April of 1764, while the Wawatams were at their sugaring area or on the coast of Lake Michigan, they probably ate considerable quantities of maple sugar. In the previous year at the same season Henry had been one of a party of eight people who consumed about 300 pounds of maple sugar in a month while producing an additional 1,600 pounds of maple sugar and 36 gallons of syrup. It thus seems likely that the Wawatam family made at least enough maple sugar to sustain them for a month and probably much more.

In the summer of 1764 the Wawatam family again engaged in fishing and hunting at St. Martin Bay. In that summer they still had some of the bear oil and strips of dried bear meat they had obtained the previous winter. They also should have had left some of their dried venison.

Using the archaeologist Wilbert B. Hinsdale's estimate of the equivalent of 1,000 pounds of dry foodstuff as the yearly requirement of an average adult (Hinsdale, 1932, p. 10), the seven adult members of the Wawatam family (including Alexander Henry) would have needed 7,000 pounds of such food in a year. In the year 1763–64 the Wawatam family must have collected an amount of food that, if weighed when dry, would have exceeded 7,000 pounds. In February alone they had 4,000 pounds of dried venison in addition to an unstated quantity cached at a former encampment. If the year 1763–64 can be considered typical, the Wawatam family did not lack food and might even have been wealthy by the standards of the time and place.

The Importance of Maple Sugar

Whatever its origin, maple sugar was an important food among the somewhat acculturated Chippewa of Alexander Henry's time. Speaking of maple sugar, Henry wrote, "I have known Indians to live wholly upon the same, and become fat" (Henry, ed. Bain, 1901, p. 71). For about one month of each year the principal part of the Indian diet was maple sugar.

The earlier part of the spring [wrote Henry] is that best adapted to making maple-sugar. The sap runs only in the day; and it will not run, unless there has been a frost the night before. When, in the morning, there is a clear sun, and the night has left ice of the thickness of a dollar, the greatest quantity is produced. (Henry, ed. Bain, 1901, p. 70.)

In late March of 1763, a time before he had become a part of the Wawatam family, Alexander Henry and seven Chippewa Indians were at a sugaring camp near Sault Ste Marie, Michigan. According to Henry,

A certain part of the maple-woods having been chosen, . . . a house, twenty feet long and fourteen broad, was begun in the morning, and before night made fit for the comfortable reception of eight persons, and their baggage.

The next day was employed in gathering the bark of white birch-trees, with which to make vessels to catch the wine or sap. The trees were now cut or tapped, and spouts or ducts introduced into the wound. The bark vessels were placed under the ducts; and, as they filled, the liquor was taken out in buckets, and conveyed into reservoirs or vats of moose-skin, each vat containing a hundred gallons [Fig. 33]. From these, we supplied the boilers, of which we had twelve, of from twelve to twenty gallons each, with fires constantly under them, day and night. While the women collected the sap, boiled it, and completed the sugar, the men were not less busy in cutting wood, making fires, hunting and fishing. . . .

.   .   .   .

On the twenty-fifth of April, our labour ended, and we returned to the [trading post], carrying with us . . . sixteen hundred [pounds] weight of sugar. We had besides, thirty-six gallons of syrup; and, during our stay in the woods, we certainly consumed three hundred weight [of maple sugar]. Though, as I have said, we hunted and fished, yet sugar was our principal food, during the whole month of April. (Henry, ed. Bain, 1901, pp. 70–71.)

In about one month in the spring of 1763 Alexander Henry and his Indians friends had produced almost one ton of maple sugar and 36 gallons of maple syrup. According to Dr. Hinsdale's estimates, about two pounds of maple sugar per day is sufficient food for one adult (Hinsdale, 1932, p. 9). On this basis the sugaring group of which Alexander Henry was a part produced enough maple sugar to sustain them for 118 days.

They must have collected tremendous quantities of maple sap. Since it takes about 50 gallons of sap to make one gallon of syrup, the 36 gallons of syrup mentioned by Henry must represent 1,800 gallons of sap. Since it also takes about 50 gallons of sap to make 8 pounds of sugar, the 1,900 pounds of sugar listed by Henry must represent some 11,875 gallons of sap (Panshin *et al.*, 1950, pp. 464–67). Thus the Chippewa Indian women in Alexander Henry's group must have collected about 13,675 gallons of maple sap in the spring of 1763.

To obtain this amount of sap it probably would have been necessary for the Indians to tap some 700 or more maple trees. And

Fig. 33. — Chippewa Indian women making maple syrup and maple sugar near Sault Ste Marie in 1762. Courtesy of Chicago Natural History Museum.

since it takes one cord of wood to produce 8 to 10 gallons of syrup in a modern evaporator, the Indians and Alexander Henry must have had to collect the equivalent of at least thirty cords of wood for their twelve boilers that had fires constantly under them day and night (Panshin *et al.*, 1950, pp. 464–67). As Henry has indicated, the men cut the wood for the fires and the women collected the maple sap and boiled it into syrup and sugar.

The transportation of the surplus sugar and syrup to their summer village or a trading post must have presented somewhat of a problem. A gallon of syrup should weigh 11 pounds; thus the 36 gallons of syrup produced by Alexander Henry and his friends should have weighed 396 pounds (Panshin *et al.*, 1950, pp. 464–67). With the weight of the syrup added to the 1,600 pounds of sugar they produced there was a total of 1,996 pounds of maple products that had to be transported by eight persons. This was a load of more than 200 pounds per person. If they also transported their sugaring kettles and other equipment they must have made several trips between their sugaring camp and the trading post at Sault Ste Marie.

The sugar and syrup produced by the Chippewa in the second half of the eighteenth century probably constituted about one-twelfth of the annual diet of many Chippewa Indians. In addition, the surplus of these products was bartered at trading posts or possibly exchanged for corn with the Ottawa. For these reasons, maple sugar and syrup were extremely important in the Chippewa economy during this period.

MATERIAL CULTURE

Of possible interest to the archaeologist is the following list of items of material culture that are mentioned by Alexander Henry in the account of his year's stay with the Wawatam family. Articles of clothing include shirts, cloth leggings, and common shoes or moccasins. Ornaments mentioned are silver armbands, silver wristbands, and a collar and necklace of wampum.

Tools mentioned are steel axes of one and a half pound weight, knives, trenching tools, and iron traps. Weapons are flintlock guns with powder and bullets. Utensils include wooden bowls (dishes), wooden spoons, flint and steel (strike-a-lights) for making fire, brass kettles, and tobacco pipes.

The only musical instrument mentioned is the drum. Items of travel and transport are the birchbark canoe, wooden paddles, burden straps, and snowshoes.

THE ARCHAEOLOGY OF THE WAWATAM FAMILY

What sort of archaeological record was left by the Wawatam family in the year 1763–64? What remnants of their culture and society would an archaeologist expect to find some two centuries later? And what activities of the Wawatam family can illuminate the interpretation of the general archaeological record that already exists in parts of the upper Great Lakes region?

First of all, the only village sites used by the Wawatam family were on Mackinac Island or at Mackinaw City. In the ordinary course of events these seem only to have been occupied in the summer. There should be an extensive archaeological record at each of these village sites. The Wawatam family, however, spent the summer of 1763 and at least part of the summer of 1764 at St. Martin Bay.

Somewhere at St. Martin Bay there should be the remains of the Wawatam family dwelling. There should be post molds, fireplaces, any objects that they discarded or lost, and food refuse represented mostly by fish and fowl. On St. Martin Island there should be a similar campsite marked by tremendous quantities of sturgeon bones and plates.

The autumn campsite of the Wawatam family some 15 miles or more inland from Lake Michigan should provide an interesting archaeological record. It was occupied for at least three months in 1763 and may have been used annually for a number of years. In addition to post molds, hearths, pits, lost or discarded artifacts, there should be food refuse with a preponderance of beaver and raccoon bone over other types of animal remains. Somewhere within the boundaries of this lodge there would be a pit that contained fourteen complete corncobs, the ritually buried remnants of a ceremony held on the night of November 1, 1763. There were two cobs for each adult; thus if two cobs were a fixed number in such ceremonies, it would be possible for an archaeologist to estimate the population of the lodge by the contents of such a pit. Outside the lodge there would be additional hearths and post molds left from the scaffolding erected to hold a cache of furs and dried meat.

The winter encampment in the interior of Michigan seems to have been occupied by the Wawatam family for about two months. It would be of interest to know if the lodge erected at this place was different from that used at the autumn encampment. A conical wigwam would seem to have been the most efficient form of dwelling for this time and place. If, in fact, the Wawatam women erected a conical wigwam on frozen ground there would remain very little evidence of this for the archaeologist to find. There would be no post molds. There should be, however, extensive remains of hearths both inside the lodge and outside for smoking meat, as well as whatever artifacts were lost or discarded, and food remnants manifesting a preponderance of elk bones.

The campsites lying between the autumn headquarters of the Wawatam family and their interior winter encampment were of two kinds. On the December 1763 march to the interior there were two campsites. At one of these they remained one night. At the other campsite they remained two days, butchering an elk and smoking the meat. The latter site should show evidence of hearths inside and outside of the lodge and elk bone refuse in the immediate vicinity. On their departure from the winter encampment there was the problem of forwarding a tremendous weight of supplies, furs, and dried meat in stages. Each staging camp might have been in use a week or more. In addition to the usual manifestations of a campsite there would have been an unusual amount of scaffolding upon which supplies were stored to protect them against wolves. An archaeologist digging such a site should find a large number of post molds, some evidence of a dwelling, and very little food refuse — perhaps none, if the Indians subsisted exclusively on their dried meat.

It is not clear whether the Wawatam family, when they returned to the vicinity of Lake Michigan, remained in their autumn camp to engage in sugaring or moved to a new place near-by. In any case they were joined at their maple groves by additional families of Indians, and their community was increased by "several lodges." This situation existed for a month or so, and the archaeologist would expect to find the remains of a substantial campsite.

If three or four families utilized the area annually there might even be enough lodge remains to suggest a village site, which in this case would be an incorrect interpretation. Food refuse at such a site would be relatively scarce because the Indians were subsisting principally on maple sugar and perhaps dried meat. An archaeologist might find the bones of fish, migrating fowl, and small animals as food refuse. There should be extensive hearth remains from all of the boiling of maple sap. If the same site were occupied in the autumn as well as in spring, the situation would be complicated for the archaeologist. A clue to this kind of situation might be found in the relative lack of bones of animals killed in winter, such as elk, plus analysis of animal bones present to see if these gave any indication of the season in which they were taken. It would be best for the archaeologist if the spring sugaring camps were entirely separate from the autumn hunting camps.

When the Wawatam family and several additional families had completed their sugar production they moved to the "border" of Lake Michigan where they remained about twenty-four days in April 1764. Their campsite could have been near the mouth of the stream or river that entered one of the estuarylike lakes in western Michigan or it could have been in the lee of sand dunes bordering the riverlike passages from the estuary lakes into Lake Michigan. In any case there should be the remains of a fair-sized encampment. An archaeologist should expect to find at such a campsite the hearths indicating the positions of the lodges, any lost or discarded artifacts, and some food refuse in which bones of fish, migratory waterfowl, and small animals predominate. At this particular campsite the archaeologist should find the bones of the "panther" that was killed by the Indians. Also, somewhere in the vicinity should be the cemetery in which the girl who died at the sugar grove was buried. The archaeologist should recover from this grave the skeleton of the girl, a steel axe head, some strings of beads, a brass or copper kettle, and if the copper salts and sand have preserved them, the remnants of a canoe paddle, snowshoes, moccasins, a burden strap, and some meat.

There remains but one more site to be considered. At the west side of the mouth of Grand Traverse Bay there was a "large party of Indians" who were joined by the Wawatam family and several other families on April 25, 1764. All of the Indians departed for L'Arbre Croche on April 26. Somewhere on the west side of Grand Traverse Bay near the mouth there should be an extensive campsite, close to the Lake Michigan shore. Chippewa Indians returning to the Straits of Mackinac region from their wintering places in the western part of the Lower Peninsula would find this a natural way station, particularly if stormy weather temporarily prevented their crossing into Grand Traverse Bay.

Although this site would have been used only for short periods in the spring and autumn and then only for transient occupancy, the site was nonetheless used by many Indians, and probably was so used for many years. On this basis the archaeologist should expect to find numerous hearths probably spread over a relatively extensive area, occasional artifacts or fragments thereof, and relatively small amounts of food refuse, among which bones of fish and migratory fowl and small mammals would predominate.

This analysis of the Wawatam family's campsites, activities, and subsistence at different times within a year offers a number of cultural clues that could be useful to an archaeologist in the interpretation of sites and settlement patterns in the Great Lakes region. It is true that the Chippewa Indians of Alexander Henry's day were considerably acculturated, but this acculturation applies primarily to material culture. And although their economic activities were tightly tied to the European fur trade they also were still linked to physical environment and the seasons, probably much as they had been in pre-European times. Thus there seems to be a continuity and conservatism of subsistence and settlement pattern that is lacking in most aspects of material culture. Because of this the Wawatam family's action in 1763–64 should cast some new light on the actions of unknown Indian families in the same region some two or three hundred years earlier.

However, what is most important at this point in the book is the insight into the culture and society of the Late Historic period that has been gained by examining the actions of the Wawatam family and Alexander Henry. In previous chapters I have shown how the archaeologist can determine through the presence of certains kinds of trade goods that cultural remains belong to a given division of the historic period, and I have indicated what kinds of cultural remains of each period have been found by excavators. The excavated materials offer invaluable clues to the rate of material acculturation, but for some purposes they are less useful than eyewitness accounts. Alexander Henry's observations as a participant in the life of the Wawatam family in 1763–64 help to round out the picture of tribal culture as it existed among the Chippewa of the marginal northern lands in the Great Lakes region. And it was this Chippewa culture that became a kind of Pan-Indian culture for the whole region, primarily because the fur trade inaugurated by Europeans was best suited to the aboriginal mode of life of the Chippewa.

References

Henry, ed. Bain, 1901 (this edition checked against Henry, 1809, and Quaife, 1921); Hinsdale, 1932; Panshin et al., 1950; Quimby, 1962.

REFERENCE MATTER

APPENDIX 1

GLASS BEADS FROM SAINTE MARIE I AND OSSOSSANE

Ste Marie I, excavated by Kenneth E. Kidd, of the Royal Ontario Museum, was the site of a former French mission on the Wye River near Midland, Ontario. Founded in 1639 by the Jesuits as a center for their activities among the Huron, Ste Marie I lasted until 1649, when it was destroyed (Kidd, 1949, p. 3). The styles of glass trade beads found in the excavation of this site (Kidd, 1949, pp. 140–42) were as follows:

1. Long tubular beads with square cross section, ¼ inch in diameter and about ½ to 2½ inches long, color opaque and like red slate or dull red brick. Ends of this type of bead are unfinished, indicating beads were broken from exceedingly long tube or cane.

2. The same style of bead with spiral S-twist.

3. Short tubular beads with round cross section, ⅛ to ¼ inch in diameter and ¼ to ⅜ inch long, color opaque and like red slate or dull red brick. Ends are unfinished.

4. Small round beads ⅛ to ¼ inch in diameter with opaque dull coral red exterior and a core of colorless glass that looks black on casual inspection because of masking effect of outer layer of red. This style is known as Cornaline d'Aleppo.

5. Small round beads ⅛ to ¼ inch in diameter that are opaque dull coral red throughout.

6. Small globular beads ³⁄₁₆ to ⁵⁄₁₆ inch in diameter and ³⁄₁₆ to ¼ inch in length, opaque dark blue or opaque light blue in color.

7. Small ovate-oblong blue beads similar to those described above.

8. Long tubular beads, round in cross section, ¼ inch in diameter and about 1¼ inches long, with spiral grooves, opaque blue color.

The Ossossane ossuary in Simcoe County, Ontario, was also excavated by Kenneth E. Kidd (1953, pp. 359–79). This mass burial consisted of the skeletal remains of about one thousand Huron Indians who died between 1624 and 1636. The actual burial ceremony took place in May of 1636 and was witnessed by the Jesuit priest, Jean Brébeuf, who recorded his observations. The types of glass beads found with the burials (Kidd, 1953, p. 369 and Fig. 123) were as follows:

1. Long tubular beads with square cross section about ¼ inch in diameter and ½ to 3 inches long, of opaque dull brick red color. Ends of beads are unfinished.

2. The same style of bead with spiral S-twist.

3. Long tubular beads with triangular cross section, without twist, but otherwise similar to the above-mentioned red tubular beads.

4. Small round beads about ⅜ inch in diameter with opaque red exterior and colorless core, Cornaline d'Aleppo style.

5. Small round beads about ¼ inch in diameter that are of opaque blue color.

6. Small elliptical beads (football shape) ⅜ inch long and opaque white in color.

7. Polychrome chevron or star beads, barrel-shaped about ½ inch in diameter and ½ inch in length. The canes by which these beads are formed were built up of concentric layers — deep cobalt blue, opaque brick red, opaque white, and sometimes other colors, in six or more bands. The main layers are divided by thinner ones, and the dividing surfaces are worked into a series of zigzags producing a chevron effect at the ends of the beads and a starlike pattern in cross section.

8. Polychrome oval beads about ½ inch long of opaque brick red color with three vertical opaque white stripes, in each of which is an opaque blue stripe.

9. Polychrome oval beads about ⅜ to ½ inch in length, of opaque light blue color with three vertical opaque white stripes.

APPENDIX 2

GLASS BEADS FROM HURON AND PETUN SITES

In the collections of the Royal Ontario Museum at Toronto, Canada, there are glass beads from various Huron and Petun sites in Ontario. As explained elsewhere such beads must represent the period from about 1600 to not later than 1650, otherwise they could not have been associated with Huron artifacts in that region. The following types of glass beads were among those observed by me in the Royal Ontario Museum's collections:

1. Long tubular beads of opaque brick red color, square or round in cross section, of same style already described in Appendix 1.

2. Similar beads of opaque blue, round section.

3. Small round beads with opaque red exterior and colorless core, Cornaline d'Aleppo style.

4. Small round beads similar in size and shape to Cornaline d'Aleppo style but opaque red color throughout.

5. Small round beads of opaque dark or light blue.

6. Small round beads of opaque white.

7. Small elliptical or football-shaped beads of opaque white.

8. Polychrome chevron or star beads, oval and barrel-shaped

with rounded rim. Colors of opaque deep blue, opaque brick red, and opaque white. Size ranges from ½ to 1½ inches in diameter and from ½ to 1½ inches in length.

9. Polychrome round and oval beads of opaque brick red with vertical opaque white stripes, in each of which is an opaque blue stripe.

10. Similar beads that have been flattened to produce a flat ovoid form with white and blue stripes on obverse and reverse.

11. Short tubular beads of opaque brick red with three opaque white stripes, in each of which is centered a blue stripe.

12. Polychrome oval and round beads of opaque blue with three vertical opaque white stripes.

APPENDIX 3

GLASS BEADS FROM A NEUTRAL SITE

In 1837 many glass beads and various artifacts were excavated from neutral Indian burials at Beverly, near Dundas, Ontario, by curiosity-seekers and pioneer pot-hunters. Neutral contact with the French began shortly after A.D. 1600, and by 1650 the Neutral had been driven from the area by the Iroquois; therefore the beads from the Beverly ossuaries must date between 1600 and 1650. Henry R. Schoolcraft (1853, I, 103–4, Plates 8, 9, 24, 25; and 1857, VI, 603, Plate 25) obtained data concerning the site and some of the glass beads and other artifacts.

The glass beads illustrated by Schoolcraft include long tubular beads of opaque brick red, either round or square in cross section, a similar bead with square cross section and a spiral S-twist, large polychrome chevron or star beads, long tubular beads of opaque blue with round or square cross sections, a long tubular bead of opaque blue with vertical white stripes, and some short cylindrical monochrome and polychrome beads with unfinished ends. These short cylindrical beads look as if they had been made by breaking more or less standardized segments from a continuous tube that already had all of the characteristics of these beads except size. The monochrome beads of this class were opaque dark blue, opaque light blue, opaque white, and opaque brick red. The polychrome beads were opaque blue with vertical stripes of opaque white, opaque blue with spiral stripes of opaque white, and opaque white with spiral stripes of opaque red, in each of which is centered an opaque blue stripe.

APPENDIX 4

GLASS BEADS FROM OLD FORT ALBANY

The glass beads excavated from Old Fort Albany by Walter A. Kenyon are in the collections of the Royal Ontario Museum. Old Fort Albany was built in 1680 and destroyed in 1715; therefore the beads associated with its ruins must have been at the fort sometime between 1680 and 1715. These glass beads include the following types:

1. Long tubular beads of opaque blue about ¾ to 1½ inches long.

2. Elongate spheroidal beads ³⁄₁₆ to ⅜ inch in diameter and ⅜ to ⅝ inch long of opaque white. These beads usually have a nib or slight projection at the line hole.

3. Small football-shaped beads about ⅜ inch long of opaque bluish green.

4. Small round beads of opaque bluish green about ¼ inch in diameter.

5. Oblate spheroidal beads of opaque blue about ⅜ inch in diameter.

6. Elongate spheroidal beads of opaque blue about ⅜ inch in diameter and ½ inch in length.

7. Oblate spheroidal beads about ⅜ inch in diameter of opaque

brick red with translucent colorless cores that appear to be black on casual inspection. This is the Cornaline d'Aleppo style.

8. Elongate spheroidal beads of the same style about ½ inch in length.

9. Large oblate spheroidal beads of shiny black about ½ inch in diameter.

10. Small round and oblate spheroidal beads of opaque white about ¼ inch in diameter.

11. Small round or oblate spheroidal beads of opaque blue about ⅛ to ¼ inch in diameter.

12. Small oblate spheroidal shiny black beads about ¼ inch in diameter.

13. Small oblate spheroidal beads about ¼ inch in diameter, of opaque dull red exterior with core of translucent colorless glass that looks black on casual inspection. This is a Cornaline d'Aleppo style.

14. Long tubular polychrome beads of opaque blue with vertical (parallel to line hole) white stripes. These beads are about 1 inch in length, and round in cross section.

15. Long tubular polychrome beads about 1 inch long of opaque white with two spiraling stripes of opaque reddish brown.

16. Elongate spheroidal polychrome beads about ½ inch long of opaque white with three vertical stripes of opaque brick red.

17. Large oblate spheroidal polychrome beads about ⅜ to ½ inch in diameter and of opaque black with three wavy stripes of opaque white placed horizontally (at right angles to the direction of the line hole).

Numbers 2, 16, and 17 are diagnostic of the Middle Historic period, particularly of the first half of it. Probably the bugle or tubular beads, numbers 1, 14, and 15, are also diagnostic of the early part of the Middle Historic period.

APPENDIX 5

GLASS BEADS FROM THE FATHERLAND SITE AND FROM THE FORT ST. JOSEPH AREA

The following description of beads from the Fatherland site and the Fort St. Joseph area is one that I completed in 1941. However, I have recently checked it against photographs of beads from each of the collections.

SEED BEADS (VERY SMALL BEADS)

Colorless

Colorless, translucent, oblate spheroidal and tubular glass beads with diameters from ⅛ inch and lengths from ⅛ to ³⁄₁₆ inch.

Monochrome

Blue-green, oblate spheroidal and tubular glass beads with diameters from ¹⁄₁₆ to ³⁄₁₆ inch and lengths from ¹⁄₁₆ to ³⁄₁₆ inch.

Polychrome

Cornaline d'Aleppo type, red opaque with translucent bluish center, oblate spheroidal glass beads about ⅛ inch in diameter and about ⅛ inch in length.

ELONGATE SPHEROIDAL BEADS

Colorless

Colorless, translucent, elongate spheroidal glass beads with diameters from $\frac{3}{16}$ to $\frac{5}{16}$ inch and lengths from $\frac{3}{8}$ to $\frac{9}{16}$ inch.

Monochrome

Milky-white, somewhat translucent, elongate spheroidal glass bead with a diameter of $\frac{5}{8}$ inch and a length of $1\frac{1}{16}$ inches.

White, opaque, elongate spheroidal glass beads with diameters from $\frac{3}{16}$ to $\frac{3}{8}$ inch and lengths from $\frac{3}{8}$ to $\frac{5}{8}$ inch.

Gray-blue, opaque, elongate spheroidal glass beads with diameters from $\frac{3}{16}$ to $\frac{3}{8}$ inch and lengths from $\frac{3}{8}$ to $\frac{5}{8}$ inch.

Dark blue, opaque, elongate spheroidal glass beads with diameters from $\frac{3}{16}$ to $\frac{3}{8}$ inch and lengths from $\frac{3}{8}$ to $\frac{5}{8}$ inch.

Polychrome

Green, translucent, elongate spheroidal glass beads with eight inlaid white bars parallel to the line hole. The diameters range from $\frac{1}{4}$ to $\frac{3}{8}$ inch and the lengths from $\frac{3}{8}$ to $\frac{1}{2}$ inch.

Gray-blue, opaque, elongate spheroidal glass beads with three inlaid bars parallel to the line hole. These bars have white margins with red centers. The diameters range from $\frac{3}{16}$ to $\frac{5}{16}$ inch and the lengths from $\frac{3}{8}$ to $1\frac{3}{16}$ inch.

Blue, opaque, elongate spheroidal glass beads with three inlaid bars parallel to the line hole. These bars have white margins and red centers. The diameters range from $\frac{1}{8}$ to $\frac{3}{8}$ inch and the lengths from $\frac{3}{8}$ to $\frac{3}{4}$ inch.

Black, opaque, elongate spheroidal glass beads with three white inlaid bars parallel to the line hole. The diameters range from $\frac{1}{8}$ to $\frac{3}{8}$ inch and lengths from $\frac{3}{8}$ to $\frac{5}{8}$ inch.

Blue, translucent, elongate spheroidal glass beads with five white inlaid spiral bars. The diameters range from $\frac{1}{4}$ to $\frac{3}{8}$ inch and lengths from $\frac{3}{8}$ to $\frac{9}{16}$ inch.

White, opaque, elongate spheroidal glass beads with three spiral bands, each composed of three inlaid blue bars. The diameters range from $\frac{1}{4}$ to $\frac{3}{8}$ inch and the lengths from $\frac{1}{2}$ to $\frac{5}{8}$ inch.

White, opaque, elongate spheroidal glass beads with six inlaid red spiral bars. The diameters average about $\frac{1}{4}$ inch and the lengths range from $\frac{3}{8}$ to $\frac{5}{8}$ inch.

White, opaque, elongate spheroidal glass beads with six inlaid blue spiral bars. The diameters range from $\frac{1}{4}$ to $\frac{3}{8}$ inch and the lengths from $\frac{3}{8}$ to $\frac{13}{16}$ inch.

White, opaque, elongate spheroidal glass beads with three inlaid bars parallel to the line hole. The borders of these bars are red and the centers are blue. The diameters range from $\frac{3}{16}$ to $\frac{5}{16}$ inch and the lengths from $\frac{1}{4}$ to $\frac{11}{16}$ inch.

White, opaque, elongate spheroidal glass beads with three inlaid bars parallel to the line hole. These bars are blue at the margins and red in the center. The diameters range from $\frac{1}{8}$ to $\frac{1}{4}$ inch and the lengths from $\frac{3}{8}$ to $\frac{5}{8}$ inch.

White, opaque, elongate spheroidal glass beads with three inlaid blue bars parallel to the line hole. The diameters range from $\frac{1}{4}$ to $\frac{3}{8}$ inch and the lengths from $\frac{7}{16}$ to $\frac{9}{16}$ inch.

White, opaque, elongate spheroidal glass beads with six inlaid bars parallel to the line hole. These bars in repeating order are red, blue, and green. The diameters average about $\frac{5}{16}$ inch and the lengths about $\frac{9}{16}$ inch.

Spheroidal and Oblate Spheroidal Beads

Colorless

Colorless, translucent, spheroidal and oblate spheroidal glass beads with diameters from $\frac{5}{16}$ to $\frac{3}{8}$ inch and lengths from $\frac{5}{16}$ to $\frac{3}{8}$ inch.

Monochrome

White, opaque, spheroidal and oblate spheroidal glass beads with diameters from $\frac{1}{4}$ to $\frac{3}{8}$ inch and lengths from $\frac{3}{16}$ to $\frac{5}{16}$ inch.

Dark blue, opaque, spheroidal and oblate spheroidal glass beads with diameters from $\frac{1}{4}$ to $\frac{3}{8}$ inch and lengths from $\frac{3}{16}$ to $\frac{5}{16}$ inch.

Green, opaque, spheroidal and oblate spheroidal glass beads with diameters from $\frac{3}{16}$ to $\frac{5}{16}$ inch and lengths from $\frac{5}{16}$ to $\frac{3}{8}$ inch.

Polychrome

Colorless, translucent, spheroidal and oblate spheroidal glass beads with seven white threads pressed in the glass parallel to the line hole. "Gooseberry type." The diameters are about $\frac{3}{8}$ inch and the lengths vary from $\frac{5}{16}$ to $\frac{7}{16}$ inch.

Cornaline d'Aleppo type, reddish brown exterior shell over

core of opaque blue. The shape is spheroidal. The diameters are about ⁵⁄₁₆ inch and the lengths are also about ⁵⁄₁₆ inch.

Blue, translucent, spheroidal and oblate spheroidal glass beads with eight white inlaid bars parallel to the line hole. The diameters are from ¼ to ⅜ inch and the lengths from ³⁄₁₆ to ⅜ inch.

Green, translucent, spheroidal glass beads with eight inlaid white bars parallel to the line hole. The diameters are about ⁵⁄₁₆ inch and the lengths are also ⁵⁄₁₆ inch.

White, opaque, spheroidal glass beads with three bars parallel to the line hole. These bars have red margins and blue centers. The diameters are about ⁵⁄₁₆ inch, and the lengths are also ⁵⁄₁₆ inch.

Black, opaque, oblate spheroidal glass beads with a network of three wavy stripes of white or yellowish white inlay placed horizontally. The diameters are from ⅜ to ½ inch and the lengths from ⁵⁄₁₆ to ⁷⁄₁₆ inch.

Oblate Spheroidal Joined Beads

Monochrome

White, opaque, oblate spheroidal joined glass beads with diameters of ⁵⁄₁₆ to ⅜ inch and lengths of ½ to ⁹⁄₁₆ inch.

Blue-gray, opaque, oblate spheroidal joined glass beads with diameters of ⁵⁄₁₆ to ⅜ inch and lengths of ½ to ⁹⁄₁₆ inch.

Polychrome

Black, opaque, oblate spheroidal joined glass beads with a network of three intertwined white or yellowish white bands. The diameters average ⅜ inch and the lengths about ⁹⁄₁₆ inch.

Spheroidal Fluted Beads

Blue, translucent, spheroidal glass beads with longitudinal fluting. Diameters are about ⅜ inch and lengths are about ⅜ inch.

Decahedral Beads (also called beads with eight facets)

Colorless, translucent, decahedral glass beads with diameters of about ⅜ inch and lengths from ⅜ to ½ inch.

Blue, somewhat opaque, decahedral glass beads with diameters of about ⅜ inch and lengths from ⅜ to ½ inch. These beads have eight facets and are ten-sided when one counts the flat ends.

Raspberry-shaped Beads

Colorless, translucent, raspberry-shaped glass beads with diameters of ⅜ inch and lengths also about ⅜ inch.

Blue, translucent, raspberry-shaped glass beads with diameters of about ⅜ inch and lengths also about ⅜ inch.

APPENDIX 6

MAKERS OF TRADE SILVER AND THEIR MARKS

In the following pages there are listed many of the silversmiths who are known to have produced silver ornaments for the Indian trade. The listing is by country.

ENGLISH SILVERSMITHS

Silver ornaments for trade with Indians were made by a number of London silversmiths. Among them were Peter Arno, *ca.* 1768, whose maker's mark consisted of the roman letters "AR" in a shield-shaped cartouche (Brannon, 1935, p. 81); Hester Bateman, *ca.* 1771–1781, whose mark (Fig. 21, A) consisted of the script letters "HB" in a rectangular cartouche; William Evans, *ca.* 1761–1774 (Gillingham, 1938); the firm of George Heming and William Chawner, *ca.* 1781, whose stamp consisted of the roman letters "GH" over "WC" in a square cartouche (Quimby, 1938, p. 67); Benjamin Laver, *ca.* 1781, whose maker's mark consisted of the roman letters "BL" in a rectangular cartouche (Quimby, 1937, p. 22); and Luke Kendall, *ca.* 1775, whose maker's mark (Fig. 21, P) consisted of the roman letters "LK" in a rectangular cartouche.

The date letters in the hallmarks of London silversmiths indicate that the silver ornaments were made from at least 1763 to 1805.

CANADIAN SILVERSMITHS

Silver ornaments stamped with the script letters "RC" in a curvilinear cartouche (Fig. 21, B and C) were made by Robert
Cruickshank, a silversmith and merchant of Montreal. Various
documentary records show that Cruickshank's period of produc-
tivity in Montreal lasted from about 1779 to 1806 or perhaps
1809 (Barbeau, 1940; Quimby, 1937; and Traquair, 1938).
Therefore, trade silver bearing the maker's stamp of Robert Cruickshank can be dated at not earlier than the last quarter of the
eighteenth century.

The maker's mark consisting of the script letters "CA" in a
curvilinear cartouche (Fig. 21, D) is that of Charles Arnoldi,
another silversmith of Montreal. Documentary evidence dates the
work of Charles Arnoldi from at least 1784 to 1810 (Barbeau,
1940; Quimby, 1937; and Traquair, 1938).

Silver ornaments stamped with the roman letters "PH" in an
oblong cartouche (Fig. 21, E) were made by Pierre Huguet dit
Latour, a silversmith and merchant of Montreal. Various records
date the work of Pierre Huguet dit Latour in the period from
1770 to 1816 (Barbeau, 1940; and Traquair, 1938).

Another important merchant and silversmith of Montreal was
Narcisse Roy. His mark (Fig. 21, H) stamped on silver ornaments
consisted of the script letters "NR" in trapezoidal cartouche. Documentary evidence shows that Narcisse Roy was supplying silver
ornaments for the Indian trade from at least 1801 to 1806 (Barbeau, 1940).

The stamped maker's mark consisting of the roman letters "JO"
in a square or rectangular cartouche (Fig. 21, G) was probably
that of John Oakes, who was a Montreal silversmith and a onetime
associate of Charles Arnoldi (Quimby, 1937; and Traquair,
1938). Oakes's association with Arnoldi suggests that he practiced his craft sometime in the period from at least 1784 to 1810.

The maker's stamp consisting of the roman letters "CG" in a
rectangular cartouche (Fig. 21, N) probably was the mark of
Christian Grothe, a silversmith who was known to have worked
in Montreal in 1795.

Some other Montreal silversmiths who are known or believed
to have produced silver ornaments for the Indian trade in the
last quarter of the eighteenth and the first quarter of the nine-

teenth century are the following: Peter Arnoldi, whose maker's mark probably consisted of the roman letters "PA" in a square cartouche; Michel Arnoldi; David Bohle; Peter Bohle, whose maker's mark may have been the roman letters "PB" in a rectangular cartouche; Curtius; Comens; Sam Flint; C. Le Claire; Solomon Marion, whose mark probably consisted of the roman letters "SM" in a rectangular cartouche; Jos. Normandeau; Henri Polonceau; Jonathan Tyler, whose maker's mark probably was a rectangular cartouche enclosing the roman letters "JT"; and Webster.

Some maker's marks accompanied by the word "Montreal" stamped on the same piece of silver are indicative of the work of unidentified Montreal silversmiths. Some of these marks are the following: the script letters "JH" in a curvilinear cartouche; the roman letter "H" in a rectangular cartouche; and the roman letters "CF" in a rectangular cartouche. The mark consisting of the roman letters "HS" in a rectangular cartouche (Fig. 21, J) may also belong in this category.

Although the word "Montreal" in a long rectangular cartouche has occasionally occurred in conjunction with the maker's marks of many of the leading silversmiths of Montreal, it also occurs alone and may of itself, in such cases, be considered the maker's mark (Fig. 21, I).

It would appear that the greater number of Canadian silversmiths were located in Montreal. However, there were a few elsewhere; for instance, Quebec had Delagrave, Ranvoyze, the Schindlers, and Sasseville.

Jonas Schindler and, after his death, his wife, who then became known as Widow Schindler, were silversmiths who between them made silver ornaments from at least 1779 to 1802. The mark (Fig. 21, M) consisting of the roman letters "IS" in an oblong of an oval cartouche is probably the stamp of the Schindlers (Barbeau, 1940; Traquair, 1938).

The maker's mark consisting of the roman letters "FD" in a rectangular cartouche probably is that of François Delagrave, who is known to have been working in Quebec in 1826 (Barbeau, 1940).

François Ranvoyze, 1739 to 1819, had the stamped "FR" in relief but without cartouche (Barbeau, 1940).

There are a few unidentified maker's marks that seem to be those of Canadian silversmiths because they appear on groups of ornaments that are in recurring associations with ornaments known to have been made by Canadian silversmiths. Some examples are the roman letters or numerals "XII" or "IXII" or "IXIII" in a rectangular cartouche and the script letters "WC" in a curvilinear cartouche (Fig. 21, F and L).

Sandwich, Ontario, in 1808 had at least one silversmith, Augustin Lagrave, and perhaps another, Pierre Riople, who was a polisher of silver, if not actually a smith.

In the late eighteenth century Canada seems to have been the center for the production of silver ornaments for the Indian trade; most of the ornaments found in the Great Lakes region were made by Canadian silversmiths. Moreover, American trading companies in competition with those of Canada apparently found it advantageous to buy Canadian silver, for in 1797 Jacob Astor and Co. were buying silver ornaments from the Widow Schindler through the Canadian company of J. and A. McGill (Traquair, 1938). Two years later, in 1799, perhaps in an effort to obtain some of the Astor business, a New York silversmith named M. Letourneaux advertised in a local newspaper as follows: "He informs all merchants, traders, etc., to the interior of the United States of America, that having spent several years in Canada he is perfectly acquainted with such ornamental manufacture . . . as are adapted to the modern tastes of the Indian Natives of the various tribes, not only in a style to gratify their vanity, but to advance a more important object to those concerned with the furskin trade" (Ensko, 1937, p. 96). Another silversmith who learned his craft in Canada was John Kinzie, who made silver ornaments for the fur trade from 1780 to about 1812, while living first in Detroit and later in Chicago.

SILVERSMITHS IN THE UNITED STATES

Though Canada led the field, there were silversmiths in the United States as well, and the following are some of those who worked in the Northwest Territory during the last quarter of the eighteenth century and the first part of the nineteenth century:

John Kinzie, who is better known as a Chicago pioneer than as a silversmith, made silver ornaments for the fur trade for over thirty years. Kinzie became apprenticed to a silversmith in Quebec about 1774. From 1781 to 1812 he combined his silversmithing with the fur trade in a number of different places within the Northwest Territory. Kinzie's maker's mark (Fig. 21, o) probably consisted of the script letters "JK" in a rectangular cartouche (Quimby, 1937).

Peter John (Pierre Jean) Desnoyers, a silversmith born in France in 1772, was working in Detroit from at least 1818 to 1837. Possibly Desnoyers is the maker of silver ornaments that bear a stamp consisting of the roman letters "PJD" in a serrated rectangular cartouche or a plain rectangular cartouche.

Jean Baptiste Bequette was silversmith in Fort Wayne from at least 1820 to 1823. He employed some forty helpers in his silversmithing establishment. Probably Bequette is the manufacturer of silver ornaments that bear the maker's mark consisting of the roman letters "JBB" in a rectangular cartouche (Gillingham, 1938; Quimby, 1937; Woodward, 1938, p. 55).

A substantial number of eastern silversmiths supplied silver ornaments for use in the fur trade. Some Philadelphia silversmiths who made such ornaments were John Bayly, *ca.* 1761, who may have owned the mark consisting of the roman letters "JB" separated by a leaf and a rectangular cartouche with a serrated base; John Baptiste Dumoutet, *ca.* 1790 to 1800; John David, Jr., *ca.* 1792 to 1800, whose mark consisted of the roman letters "JD" in an oval cartouche; John Dupuy, *ca.* 1792 to 1800, whose mark consisted of the roman letters "JD" in a rectangular cartouche; John Leacock, who is known to have made ornaments *ca.* 1776 to 1796; William Hollingshead, *ca.* 1760; Edmund Milne, 1757 to 1813, whose mark consisted of the roman letters "EM" in an oval or rectangular cartouche; Benjamin Price, *ca.* 1767, whose mark may have been the roman letters "BP" in a square cartouche; Joseph Richardson, who made ornaments from 1759 to about 1795 and whose mark consisted of the roman letters "IR" in a rectangular cartouche; Joseph Richardson, Jr., *ca.* 1777 to 1805, whose mark consisted of the roman letters "JR" in a rectangular cartouche; and Philip Syng, *ca.* 1760, whose mark consisted of the roman letters "PS" in a square cartouche, sometimes with a star or leaf additional (Gillingham, 1936, 1938; Quimby, 1937; and Woodward, 1938).

New York was also something of a center for silversmiths who made ornaments for the Indian trade. Some of the New York silversmiths were Frederick Becker, *ca.* 1736 and probably later; Daniel Christian Feuter, *ca.* 1754 to 1761; M. Letourneaux, *ca.* 1797 to 1799; Myer Myers, *ca.* 1767; Abraham and James Simmons, *ca.* 1805 to 1813; A. and J. Scrymgeour, whose mark probably consisted of the roman letters "A&JS" in a rectangular cartouche often accompanied by the mark, "New York" (Herrick, 1958); Daniel Van Voorhis, *ca.* 1789, whose mark consisted of the roman letters "DV" in a rectangular cartouche and a small American eagle in addition; Hugh Wishart, 1784 to 1810; and Benjamin Young, *ca.* 1769 (Alberts, 1953; Brannon, 1935; Gillingham, 1938; and Woodward, 1938 and 1945).

Some other eastern silversmiths were Charles A. Burnett of Alexandria, Virginia, 1793 to 1824, whose maker's mark consisted of the roman letters "CAB" in a rectangular cartouche; John Benjamin of Stratford, Connecticut, *ca.* 1752; Samuel Bosworth of Buffalo, 1828 to 1838; John Corbin of Stratford, Connecticut, 1750 to 1796; Joseph Loring of Boston, 1788 to 1796; James Mix of Albany, 1790 to 1817; Asa Ransom of Geneva, New York, 1789 to 1800; Robert Scott of Virginia, *ca.* 1781; and Barent Ten Eyck of Albany, *ca.* 1764 (Woodward, 1938).

REFERENCES

Alberts, 1953; Barbeau, 1940; Brannon, 1935; Ensko, 1937; Gillingham, 1936, 1938; Herrick, 1958; Kidd, 1949, 1953; Quimby, 1937; Schoolcraft, 1853, 1857; Traquair, 1938; Woodward, 1938.

BIBLIOGRAPHY

ALBERTS, ROBERT C.
  1953. "Trade Silver and Indian Silver Work in the Great Lakes region."
  Wisconsin Archaeologist, *34*, No. 1, pp. 2–121. Milwaukee.
BAERREIS, DAVID A.
  1961. "The Ethnohistoric Approach and Archaeology." *Ethnohistory*, *8*,
  No. 1, pp. 49–77. Bloomington, Indiana.
BALLARD, RALPH
  1949. *Old Fort St. Joseph.* Niles, Michigan.
BARBEAU, MARIUS
  1940. "Indian Trade Silver." *Transactions of the Royal Society of Can-
  ada*, Section II, pp. 27–41. Toronto.
  1942. "Indian Trade Silver." *The Beaver: A Magazine of the North*,
  Outfit 273 (December), pp. 10–14. Winnipeg.
BAUXAR, J JOE
  1959. "The Historic Period," in *Illinois Archaeology*. Illinois Archaeo-
  logical Survey Bulletin No. 1 (Elaine A. Bluhm, ed.), pp. 40–58.
  Carbondale.
BINFORD, LEWIS R.
  1962. "A New Method of Calculating Dates from Kaolin Pipe Stem
  Samples." *Southeastern Archaeological Conference Newsletter*, *9*,
  No. 1, pp. 19–21. Cambridge, Mass.

BINFORD, LEWIS R., AND GEORGE I. QUIMBY
   1963. *Indian Sites and Chipped Stone Materials in the Northern Lake
       Michigan Area.* Fieldiana: Anthropology, Vol. 36, No. 12. Chicago.
BLAIR, EMMA HELEN (ed.)
   1911. *The Indian Tribes of the Upper Mississippi Valley and Region
       of the Great Lakes as described by Nicolas Perrot, French Com-
       mandant in the Northwest; Bacqueville de la Potherie, French
       Royal Commissioner to Canada; Morrell Marston, American Ar-
       my Officer; and Thomas Forsyth, United States Agent at Fort
       Armstrong.* 2 vols. Cleveland.
BLUHM, ELAINE A., AND GLORIA J. FENNER
   1961. "The Oak Forest Site," in *Chicago Area Archaeology.* Illinois Ar-
       chaeological Survey Bulletin No. 3 (Elaine A. Bluhm, ed.), pp.
       138–61. Urbana.
BLUHM, ELAINE A., AND ALLEN LISS
   1961. "The Anker Site," in *Chicago Area Archaeology*, Illinois Archae-
       ological Survey Bulletin No. 3 (Elaine A. Bluhm, ed.), pp. 89–137.
       Urbana.
BRANNON, PETER A.
   1935. *The Southern Indian Trade.* Montgomery, Alabama.
BROWN, CHARLES E.
   1918. "Indian Trade Implements and Ornaments." *Wisconsin Archae-
       ologist, 17,* No. 3, pp. 61–97. Milwaukee.
EMERSON, J. NORMAN
   1961. "Cahiague 1961." Public Lecture Series, University of Toronto
       Archaeological Field School at the Cahiague Site, Simcoe County,
       Ontario. Mimeographed report prepared with the cooperation and
       assistance of the Orillia Board of Education.
ENSKO, ROBERT
   1937. *Marks of American Silversmiths.* New York.
FAIRBANKS, CHARLES H.
   1962. "European Ceramics from the Cherokee Capitol of New Echota."
       Southeastern Archaeological Conference Newsletter, 9, No. 1,
       pp. 10–16. Cambridge, Mass.
FORD, JAMES A.
   1936. *Analysis of Indian Village Site Collections from Louisiana and
       Mississippi.* Anthropological Study No. 2. Department of Conser-
       vation, Louisiana Geological Survey. New Orleans.
GILLINGHAM, HAROLD E.
   1936. *Indian Ornaments Made by Philadelphia Silversmiths.* Published
       under the auspices of the Museum of the American Indian, Heye
       Foundation. New York.
   1938. Personal communication.
   1943. "Indian Trade Silver Ornaments Made by Joseph Richardson,
       Jr." *Pennsylvania Magazine of History and Bibliography,* Janu-
       ary, pp. 83–91.

GLASGOW, TOM, JR.
1964. "The Shape of the Ships That Defeated the Spanish Armada." *Mariner's Mirror*, *50*, No. 3, pp. 177–87. Society for Nautical Research. London.

GREENMAN, EMERSON F.
1951. *Old Birch Island Cemetery and the Early Historic Trade Route, Georgian Bay, Ontario*. Occasional Contributions from the Museum of Anthropology of the University of Michigan, No. 11. Ann Arbor.
1958. "An Early Historic Cemetery at St. Ignace." *Michigan Archaeologist*, *4*, No. 2, pp. 28–35. Ann Arbor.

GRIFFIN, JAMES B.
1943. *The Fort Ancient Aspect: Its Cultural and Chronological Position in Mississippi Valley Archaeology*. Ann Arbor.

HALL, ROBERT L.
1962. *The Archeology of Carcajou Point with an Interpretation of the Development of Oneota Culture in Wisconsin*. 2 vols. Madison, Wisconsin.

HAMILTON, T. M.
1960. "Indian Trade Guns." *Missouri Archaeologist*, *22* (entire volume, compiled and arranged by T. M. Hamilton, with articles by Hamilton and others). Columbia, Missouri.

HARRINGTON, J. C.
1954. "Dating Stem Fragments of Seventeenth and Eighteenth Century Clay Tobacco Pipes." *Quarterly Bulletin, Archeological Society of Virginia*, *9*, No. 1, pp. 10–14. Charlottesville, Virginia.

HENNEPIN, LOUIS
1698. *A New Discovery of a Vast Country in America Extending above Four Thousand Miles Between New France and New Mexico with a Description of the Great Lakes, Cataracts, Rivers, Plants, and Animals: Also, the Manners, Customs, and Languages, of the several Native Indians; And the Advantage of Commerce with those different Nations. With a Continuation Giving an Account of the Attempts of the Sieur De la Salle upon the Mines of St. Barbe, etc. The Taking of Quebec by the English; With the Advantages of a Shorter Cut to China and Japan. Both Parts Illustrated with Maps and Figures, and Dedicated to His Majesty K. William. By L. Hennepin, now Resident in Holland. To which is added, Several New Discoveries in North America, not publish'd in the French Edition*. London: Printed for M. Bentley, J. Tonson, H. Bonwick, T. Goodwin, and S. Manship. 1698.

HENRY, ALEXANDER, ESQ.
1809. *Travels and Adventures in Canada and The Indian Territories Between the Years 1760 and 1776*. New York.

HENRY, ALEXANDER. Edited by JAMES BAIN.

1901. *Travels and Adventures in Canada and the Indian Territories Between the Years 1760 and 1776.* Toronto.

HERRICK, RUTH
1958. "A Report on the Ada Site, Kent County, Michigan." *Michigan Archaeologist, 4,* No. 1, pp. 1–27. Ann Arbor.

HEWITT, J. N. B.
1912. "Sauk," in *Handbook of American Indians North of Mexico,* ed. F. W. Hodge, pp. 471–80. Bureau of American Ethnology Bulletin No. 30, Part II. Washington, D.C.

HICKERSON, HAROLD
1962. *The Southwestern Chippewa: An Ethnohistorical Study.* American Anthropological Association Memoirs, No. 92. Menasha, Wisconsin.

HINSDALE, WILBERT B.
1932. *Distribution of the Aboriginal Population of Michigan.* Occasional Contributions from the Museum of Anthropology of the University of Michigan, No. 2. Ann Arbor.

HUDSON, J. PAUL
1962. "English Glass Wine Bottles of the 17th and 18th Centuries." *Southeastern Archaeological Conference Newsletter, 9,* No. 1, pp. 6–9. Cambridge, Mass.

JELINEK, ARTHUR J.
1958. "A Late Historic Burial from Berrien County." *Michigan Archaeologist, 4,* No. 3, pp. 48–51. Ann Arbor.

JOSEPHY, ALVIN M., JR., et al.
1961. *The American Heritage Book of Indians.* New York.

KIDD, KENNETH E.
1949. *The Excavation of Ste Marie I.* Toronto.
1953. "The Excavation and Historical Identification of a Huron Ossuary." *American Antiquity, 18,* No. 4, pp. 359–79. Salt Lake City.

KINIETZ, W. VERNON
1940. *The Indians of the Western Great Lakes, 1615–1760.* Occasional Contributions from the Museum of Anthropology of the University of Michigan, No. 10. Ann Arbor.

MAXWELL, MOREAU S.
1964. "Indian Artifacts at Fort Michilimackinac, Mackinaw City, Michigan." *Michigan Archaeologist, 10,* No. 2, pp. 23–30. Ann Arbor.

MAXWELL, MOREAU S., AND LEWIS H. BINFORD.
1961. *Excavation at Fort Michilimackinac, Mackinac City, Michigan, 1959 Season.* Publications of the Museum, Michigan State University, Cultural Series, Vol. 1, No. 1. Lansing.

MCDONALD, GEORGE F.
1939. Personal communication.

MCPHERRON, ALAN L.
1963. "Late Woodland Ceramics in the Straits of Mackinac." *Papers*

of the Michigan Academy of Science, Arts, and Letters, 48, 567–76. Ann Arbor.

MONTAGUE, HOWARD
1903. Old London Silver: Its History, Its Makers and Its Marks. New York.

MORISON, SAMUEL ELIOT
1925. Maritime History of Massachusetts, 1783–1860. Boston and New York.

NUTE, GRACE LEE
1931. The Voyageur. New York and London.
1959. "Three Centuries Ago." The Naturalist, 10, No. 4, pp. 3–6. Minneapolis.

OLSEN, STANLEY J.
1963. "Dating Early Plain Buttons by Their Form." American Antiquity, 28, No. 4, pp. 551–54. Salt Lake City.

OMWAKE, H. G.
1958. "Kaolin Pipes from the Schurz Site." Bulletin of the Archaeological Society of Connecticut, No. 29, pp. 3–13. New Haven.

ORCHARD, WILLIAM C.
1929. Beads and Beadwork of the American Indians. Contributions from the Museum of the American Indian, Heye Foundation, Vol. 11. New York.

OVERTON, GEORGE
1931. "Silver Ornaments from Grand Butte." Wisconsin Archaeologist, 10, No. 3, pp. 91–98. Milwaukee.

PANSHIN, A. J., E. S. HARRAR, W. J. BAKER, AND P. B. PROCTOR
1959. Forest Products: Their Sources, Production, and Utilization. New York.

PARKER, ARTHUR C.
1910. "Origin of Iroquois Silversmithing." American Anthropologist, 12, No. 3, pp. 349–57. Lancaster, Pennsylvania.

PARKMAN, FRANCIS
1894. La Salle and the Discovery of the Great West. 12th ed. Boston.

POPHAM, ROBERT E.
1950. "Late Huron Occupations of Ontario: An Archaeological Survey of Innisfil Township." Ontario History, 42, No. 2, pp. 81–90. Toronto.

POWELL, B. BRUCE
1962. "Classification of Ceramics from Historic American Sites." Southeastern Archaeological Conference Newsletter, 9, No. 1, pp. 34–45. Cambridge, Mass.

PRATT, PETER P.
1961. Oneida Iroquois Glass Trade Bead Sequence, 1585–1745. Syracuse, New York. Distributed by the Fort Stanwix Museum, Rome, New York.

QUAIFE, MILO M.
　1921. *Alexander Henry's Travels and Adventures in the Years 1760–1776.* Lakeside Classics, Vol. 19. Chicago.
QUIMBY, GEORGE I.
　1937. "Notes on Indian Trade Silver Ornaments in Michigan." *Papers of the Michigan Academy of Science, Arts, and Letters,* 22, 15–24. Ann Arbor.
　1938. "Dated Indian Burials in Michigan." *Papers of the Michigan Academy of Science, Arts, and Letters,* 23, 63–72. Ann Arbor.
　1939. "European Trade Articles as Chronological Indicators for the Archaeology of the Historic Period in Michigan." *Papers of the Michigan Academy of Science, Arts, and Letters,* 24, 25–31. Ann Arbor.
　1942. "Indian Trade Objects in Michigan and Louisiana." *Papers of the Michigan Academy of Science, Arts, and Letters,* 27, 543–51. Ann Arbor.
　1957. *The Bayou Goula Site, Iberville Parish, Louisiana.* Fieldiana: Anthropology, Vol. 47, No. 2. Chicago.
　1960. *Indian Life in the Upper Great Lakes: 11,000 B.C. to A.D. 1800.* Chicago.
　1961. "The Pic River Site," in *Lake Superior Copper and the Indians: Miscellaneous Studies of Great Lakes Prehistory* (James B. Griffin, ed.). Museum of Anthropology, University of Michigan, Anthropological Papers, No. 17, pp. 83–89. Ann Arbor.
　1962. "Alexander Henry in Central Michigan, 1763–1764." *Michigan History,* 46, No. 3, pp. 193–200. Lansing.
　1961–1963. Field notes.
RATIGAN, WILLIAM
　1960. *Great Lakes Shipwrecks and Survivals.* Grand Rapids, Michigan.
RIDLEY, FRANK
　1952. "The Huron and Lalonde Occupations of Ontario." *American Antiquity,* 17, No. 3, pp. 197–210. Salt Lake City.
　1954. "The Frank Bay Site, Lake Nipissing, Ontario." *American Antiquity,* 20, No. 1, pp. 40–50. Salt Lake City.
ROSS, HAMILTON NELSON
　1960. *La Pointe: Village Outpost.* St. Paul, Minnesota.
SCHOOLCRAFT, HENRY R.
　1853–1857. *Information Respecting the History, Condition, and Prospects of the Indian Tribes of the United States.* Vols. 1–6. Philadelphia.
SMITH, CARLYLE S.
　1961. "Identification of French Gun Flints." *Year Book of the American Philosophical Society, 1961,* pp. 419–23. Philadelphia.
SOUTH, STANLEY A.
　1962. "The Ceramic Types at Brunswick Town, North Carolina." *South-*

eastern Archaeological Conference Newsletter, 9, No. 1, pp. 1–5. Cambridge, Mass.

TRAQUAIR, RAMSAY
1938. "Montreal and the Indian Trade Silver." *Canadian Historical Review*, March, pp. 1–8. Montreal.

TUCKER, SARA JONES (comp.)
1942. *Indian Villages of the Illinois Country* (Part I, *Atlas*). Illinois State Museum Scientific Papers, Vol. 2. Springfield.

VAN DER SLEEN, W. G. N.
1963. "A Bead Factory in Amsterdam in the Seventeenth Century." *Man, 63* (November), Article 219, pp. 172–74. London.

WITTRY, WARREN L.
1963. "The Bell Site, Wn 9: An Early Historic Fox Village." *Wisconsin Archaeologist, 44*, No. 1, pp. 1–58. Lake Mills, Wisconsin.

WOODWARD, ARTHUR
1938. *A Brief History of Navajo Silversmithing*. Museum of Northern Arizona, Bulletin 14. Flagstaff.
1945. "Highlights on Indian Trade Silver." *Antiques Magazine*, June, 1945, pp. 328–31. New York.
1948. "Trade Goods of 1748." *The Beaver: A Magazine of the North*, Outfit 279 (December), pp. 3–6. Winnipeg.

WRIGHT, JAMES V.
1963. *An Archaeological Survey along the North Shore of Lake Superior*. National Museum of Canada, Anthropology Papers, Number 3. Dept. of Northern Affairs and National Resources. Ottawa.

INDEX